Cambridge Elements ≡

Elements in Metaphysics
edited by
Tuomas E. Tahko
University of Bristol

THE METAPHYSICS
OF GENDER

E. Díaz-León
Universitat de Barcelona

CAMBRIDGE
UNIVERSITY PRESS

Shaftesbury Road, Cambridge CB2 8EA, United Kingdom

One Liberty Plaza, 20th Floor, New York, NY 10006, USA

477 Williamstown Road, Port Melbourne, VIC 3207, Australia

314–321, 3rd Floor, Plot 3, Splendor Forum, Jasola District Centre,
New Delhi – 110025, India

103 Penang Road, #05–06/07, Visioncrest Commercial, Singapore 238467

Cambridge University Press is part of Cambridge University Press & Assessment,
a department of the University of Cambridge.

We share the University's mission to contribute to society through the pursuit of
education, learning and research at the highest international levels of excellence.

www.cambridge.org
Information on this title: www.cambridge.org/9781009500388

DOI: 10.1017/9781009264167

First published 2024

A catalogue record for this publication is available from the British Library

ISBN 978-1-009-50038-8 Hardback
ISBN 978-1-009-26419-8 Paperback
ISSN 2633-9862 (online)
ISSN 2633-9854 (print)

The Metaphysics of Gender

Elements in Metaphysics

DOI: 10.1017/9781009264167
First published online: December 2024

E. Díaz-León
Universitat de Barcelona
Author for correspondence: E. Díaz-León, ediazleon@ub.edu

Abstract: What is the metaphysics of gender about? Metaphysics is the study of what there is and what it is like. On this conception, questions in the metaphysics of gender would be about the existence and nature of gender. That is, the metaphysics of gender would be about whether alleged gender categories such as being a man, a woman, or an agender person are real features or kinds, and if so, what their nature is. In recent years, the metaphysics of gender has received a lot of attention and has shifted from being a rather marginal part of metaphysics to being a growing area of interest. Moreover, growing attention to the metaphysics of gender and the social domain have given rise to fruitful methodological questions about what metaphysics is about and what the best methods to pursue metaphysical inquiries are. This Element offers a survey of recent discussions of these questions.

Keywords: gender, amelioration, Díaz-León, contextualism, woman

ISBNs: 9781009500388 (HB), 9781009264198 (PB), 9781009264167 (OC)
ISSNs: 2633-9862 (online), 2633-9854 (print)

Contents

1 Introduction

What is the metaphysics of gender about? Metaphysics is the study of what there is and what it is like. On this conception, questions in the metaphysics of gender would be about the existence and nature of gender. That is, the metaphysics of gender would be about whether alleged gender categories such as being a man, a woman or an agender person are real features or kinds, and if so, what their nature is, that is to say, in virtue of what do people have those features or belong to those kinds?

In recent years, the metaphysics of gender has received a lot of attention and has shifted from being a rather marginal part of metaphysics to being a central and growing area of interest.[1] Moreover, growing attention to the metaphysics of gender (and the social domain more generally) has given rise to novel and fruitful methodological questions about the scope and the methods of metaphysics, that is, questions about what metaphysics is about and what the best methods to carry out metaphysical inquiries about the social are. For this reason, in this Element I will focus not only on questions about the metaphysics of gender but also on questions about the *meta-metaphysics* of gender (where meta-metaphysics is the project of examining what first-order questions in metaphysics are really about).

In order to narrow down the scope of our discussion and make it more manageable, in this Element I will focus mostly on the developments in the metaphysics of gender that have occurred within the subdiscipline known as *analytic feminism* (although this subdiscipline draws from, and aims to build bridges with, other disciplines).[2] In addition, I will focus mostly on recent discussions that have taken place during the last two decades or so, a period in which the metaphysics of gender within the analytic tradition has grown exponentially. The starting point of our discussion will be Sally Haslanger's (2000) groundbreaking paper entitled 'Gender and Race: (What) Are They? (What) Do We Want Them to Be?' This article offers an example of both an original account of what gender and race are and a methodological account about how to go on answering these questions. As we will see, Haslanger (2000) proposes an *ameliorative* approach to questions about the existence and the nature of gender, to wit: to focus not on what our gender terms actually mean or refer to, but rather on what they *should* mean. This approach in philosophy has

---

[1] Mikkola (2023) provides a useful survey of recent discussions in feminism about the nature of sex and gender.

[2] See Garry (2022) for an interesting discussion of the scope and the limits of analytic feminism. See also Díaz-León (forthcoming-a) for further discussion of recent developments in this subdiscipline.

more recently received the label *conceptual engineering*, which has now become commonplace.[3]

I will start this Element by explaining the influence that ameliorative (or conceptual engineering) approaches have had in the investigation on the metaphysics of gender. This influence has been varied and multifaceted, but here I will focus on a particular form it has taken, namely, an influence via *meta-metaphysical* questions. A central question in meta-metaphysics is about what first-order debates in metaphysics are really about, and what the different, competing views really disagree about. Thus, questions in the meta-metaphysics of gender are about what debates in the metaphysics of gender are about, and how we can answer them. There is a certain approach to meta-metaphysics that in my view illuminates the connection between conceptual engineering and metaphysics in a useful way, namely, the view known as *metaphysical deflationism*, which claims (in a nutshell) that debates in metaphysics are solvable by a combination of analysing what the central terms mean (or *should* mean), and empirical questions about what entities, if any, fall under those terms (under the actual or the revised meanings), and what they are like.[4] On this view, hence, ameliorative or conceptual engineering questions are the first stage in a metaphysical inquiry.

In the following section I will focus on one of the most coherent and well-developed versions of metaphysical deflationism, namely, the one recently proposed and defended by Amie Thomasson (2015, 2016, 2017, 2020). My motivation for using this meta-metaphysical approach as a starting point in our discussion is twofold. On the one hand, Thomasson's defence of metaphysical deflationism provides a cogent and plausible approach to the meta-metaphysics of gender, or so I will argue in Sections 2 and 3. And on the other hand, metaphysical deflationism offers a clear view about what is the connection between *semantic* questions about the meaning of a central term (or the content of the corresponding concept) in a debate, and *metaphysical* questions about the nature of the corresponding phenomenon in the vicinity. In the philosophy of gender, these two questions (semantic questions and metaphysical questions) are widely discussed in a parallel way. Some philosophers are interested in drawing a connection between the two,[5] whereas other

---

[3] See Cappelen (2018) and Burgess, Cappelen, and Plunkett (2020) for useful discussions of foundational issues about conceptual engineering.

[4] Some important sources are Chalmers (2009) and Thomasson (2015).

[5] A central example here is Haslanger (2000, 2006), who clearly makes amelioration central for the metaphysics of gender. However, her own approach to meta-metaphysics is different from metaphysical deflationism, since whereas metaphysical deflationism draws on a Carnapian model (see Thomasson 2015), Haslanger is more Quinean, rejecting the analytic/synthetic distinction (see Haslanger 2006, 2020). But see also Haslanger (2016), which I think has many

philosophers are mostly interested in semantic questions for their own sake,[6] or metaphysical questions for their own sake.[7] However, I believe that the metaphysics of gender is one of the areas of metaphysics where the interconnection between semantic and metaphysical questions is more pressing, in part because of the richness of discussions of the semantics of gender terms, and in part because of the relevance of amelioration and conceptual engineering for metaphysics. Explaining and defending metaphysical deflationism will allow me to provide a systematic account of this connection and why it matters for the metaphysics of gender.

Thus, the plan is as follows. In the next section I will provide a tentative defence of *metaphysical deflationism* about first-order debates in metaphysics, and I will then argue that this approach in meta-metaphysics is a useful way of motivating the significance of amelioration or conceptual engineering in metaphysics. I will argue that inquiries in metaphysics start by examining what the central terms mean or should mean, and hence, amelioration plays a central role at the beginning of projects in metaphysics. One of my aims in this Element is to show the usefulness and fruitfulness of endorsing this meta-metaphysical approach with respect to questions about gender. After explaining Thomasson's views on meta-metaphysics and how they apply to questions in the metaphysics of gender (Section 3), I will examine several recent challenges to this sort of approach to the metaphysics of gender by feminist philosophers such as Robin Dembroff (2018) and Elizabeth Barnes (2020), among others (Sections 4.1 and 4.2). I will argue that those challenges do not pose insurmountable obstacles to metaphysical deflationism, as applied to the metaphysics of gender. In the second part of this Element, leaving meta-metaphysics behind and focusing on first-order issues about the nature of gender, I will focus on three different questions. First, we will examine the first-order issue of what our gender terms *should* mean (or what concepts those terms should express), that is, what Haslanger (2000) calls the *ameliorative* project (Section 5). In this section we will explore some accounts of what gender terms should mean, which have been prominent in recent debates. (And, if the arguments in the first part of this

---

points in common with Thomasson's (2020) pragmatic approach. See Díaz-León (2018) and Haslanger (2018, 2020) for further discussion of Haslanger's meta-metaphysics. I discuss this issue further in Sections 3 and 4.

[6] Some examples of works mostly concerned with the meaning of gender terms include Saul (2012), Díaz-León (2016), Laskowski (2020), Zeman (2020), and Chen (2021a, b).

[7] Some examples of this latter approach are Witt (2011), Mikkola (2016), Ásta (2018), and Jenkins (2023). Barnes (2018) and Dembroff (2018) explicitly argue for the separation of semantic questions and metaphysical questions about gender. I critically examine arguments for the separation of semantic and metaphysical questions in Section 4; and I further discuss some accounts on the metaphysics of gender that do not start by analysing the meaning of gender terms in Section 7.

Element are on the right track, ameliorative questions of this form are indispensable in order to answer questions about the metaphysics of gender. However, ameliorative questions about what gender terms should mean are interesting for their own sake, regardless of what approach to meta-metaphysics one has.) Then, in the following section we will further explore two alternative accounts of the semantics of gender terms, to wit, contextualism and semantic externalism. These two accounts are interesting in themselves. But again, our previous defence of metaphysical deflationism offers a further reason to explore these alternative semantic views, namely, I am interested in exploring what would follow concerning the *metaphysics* of gender if we assumed certain accounts of the meaning of gender terms. In particular, in Section 6.1 we will examine *contextualist* views about the meaning of gender terms, according to which the meaning of gender terms changes from context to context. And in Section 6.2, we will explore what would follow regarding the metaphysics of gender if we assumed a different account of the meaning of gender terms, namely, a *radical externalist* view where the meaning of gender terms is determined by factors that are external to us (including past historical facts), which can be outside our control. Finally, in Section 7, I will survey some additional accounts on the metaphysics of gender that do not necessarily start by analysing the semantics of gender terms, but rather aim to describe the nature of gender directly. I will examine the methods they use as well as the virtues of the accounts, taken as answers to first-order questions in the metaphysics of gender. As we will see, there are good reasons to favour a pluralist account about the metaphysics of gender.

In this way, we will have a survey of views about both the semantics of gender terms (which according to metaphysical deflationism is a first step in a metaphysical inquiry about gender), and the metaphysics of gender (which, as we will see, can be examined from different starting points). Interestingly, all these debates seem to point towards pluralism about gender. As I said, we will first explore the explicitly ameliorative question of what gender terms *should* mean. Of course, the ultimate goal of an ameliorative approach is to examine which gender concepts we *should* use (or what we should mean by gender terms), but in order to ascertain this, it is useful also to figure out, to the extent that we can, what gender concepts we *actually* use (that is, what concepts our gender terms actually express), since one of the considerations in order to ascertain what concepts we should use is that we want to facilitate communication, and with respect to this goal, departing very widely from our ordinary concepts has a cost. For this reason, I will examine the two different approaches to the semantics of gender terms that I have mentioned, namely, the contextualist view and the externalist view, and I will argue that in spite of appearances, they both yield similar conclusions about what our gender terms actually mean. Indeed, as we will see, I will conclude that questions about what our terms *actually* mean and what our terms *should* mean are strongly connected. In fact, it could be argued that there are no purely descriptive questions about what our terms actually mean, since normative considerations are always present (if we want to reach an answer). The difference between the two might be a matter of degree rather than a substantive one. In this way, we will conclude that questions about what gender terms actually mean depend on complex normative considerations that we have to face, no matter whether we are interested in descriptive or ameliorative questions, and within those, no matter whether we are more sympathetic to contextualist accounts or externalist accounts. On all these approaches, the final answer depends on which normative considerations we take to be more central. Hence, the semantics of gender terms ultimately depends on these normative considerations (and if one believes, as I do, that questions in the metaphysics of gender in part depend on questions in the semantics of gender terms, then it follows that questions in the metaphysics of gender depend on those central normative considerations). On this view, questions about what gender really is cannot be answered from a neutral point of view. It does not make sense to say what gender really is, independently of our aims, goals, and values.[8]

2 Descriptive versus Ameliorative Projects

Haslanger (2000) set the agenda for discussions about the metaphysics of gender (and race) for decades to come. In this milestone article, she distinguished between three different approaches to philosophical questions of the form 'What is X?' such as 'what is knowledge?' or 'what is justice?'. As Haslanger explains, philosophers could be interested in three different things when they pose questions of that form. First, they could be interested in what

---

[8] This point is especially significant because advocates of gender-critical feminism (a position that holds that trans women are not women) often claim that they just want to describe *reality* as it is. For example, Stock (2021) entitled her book *Material Girls: Why Reality Matters for Feminism*; and Joyce (2021) entitled hers *Trans: When Ideology Meets Reality*. Those titles are intended to send the subtle message that somehow, pro-trans allies have a distorted conception of reality. (Stock's book cover depicts a girl who is blindfolded.) Well, according to metaphysical deflationism (a position that was developed in mainstream metaphysics with the aim of making sense of metaphysical debates in many different areas), in order to offer an accurate description of reality, we have to start by analysing what our terms mean or *should* mean, and as we will see, it is indispensable to appeal to values and goals of the inquiry to pursue those projects. Hence, when gender-critical advocates claim that they are merely describing reality, what they are doing is to claim that their *preferred* ways of classifying reality and the underlying *values* that motivate those descriptive projects are well justified, from a normative point of view, which is a claim that needs normative support.

she calls the *conceptual* project, that is, the project of figuring out the contours of the ordinary concept associated with the term 'X' (what Haslanger 2006 called the *manifest* concept, which is the concept that would more easily come to mind if we were asked 'what is X?'). Second, they could be interested in what she called the *descriptive* project, that is, the project of figuring out what is the objective type, if any, that our term 'X' tracks (what Haslanger 2006 called the *operative* concept). This can be figured out only empirically. Third, philosophers could be interested in what Haslanger (2000) called the *analytical* project (and Haslanger 2006 called the *ameliorative* project, which is the label that stuck), which is not about the concept that we are actually expressing with our terms but rather about the concept that we *ought* to employ, that is, what our terms should mean, given certain (legitimate) aims and goals. In her view, the questions pertaining to the ameliorative project are as follows: what is the point of having this concept? Are these purposes legitimate? What concept would best serve these (legitimate) aims? Haslanger called this the *target* concept.

In particular, Haslanger's proposed concept of gender is the following:

> A group G is a gender (in context C) iff$_{df}$ its members are similarly positioned as along some social dimension (economic, political, legal, social, etc.) (in C) and the members are 'marked' as appropriately in this position by observed or imagined bodily features presumed to be evidence of reproductive capacities or function. (2003: 8)

And, relatedly, she proposed the following ameliorative analyses of the gender categories corresponding to 'man' and 'woman':

> *S is a woman* (in context C) iff$_{df}$ S is systematically subordinated along some dimension (economic, political, legal, social, etc.) (in C) and the members are 'marked' as a target for this treatment by observed or imagined bodily features presumed to be evidence of a female's reproductive biological role in reproduction.

> *S is a man* (in context C) iff$_{df}$ S is systematically privileged along some dimension (economic, political, legal, social, etc.) (in C) and the members are 'marked' as a target for this treatment by observed or imagined bodily features presumed to be evidence of a male's reproductive biological role in reproduction. (2000: 39)

As Haslanger (2000) explains, one of the objectives of these analyses is to make salient the hierarchical social structures of privilege and discrimination that we are subject to in virtue of being perceived or imagined to have a male or female role in reproduction. Even if these are not the concepts that ordinary speakers associate with the terms 'man' and 'woman', these analyses illuminate the social structures that have explanatory potential in explaining our social positions. For this reason, Haslanger (2000) advocated for an *amelioration* (or revision) of the meaning of our gender terms, so that they would come to express these new concepts.

The notion of an ameliorative project in philosophy has become extremely influential. Haslanger's work on ameliorative analyses of gender and race has given rise to a multitude of ameliorative projects in many other areas. Alexis Burgess and David Plunkett (2013a, b) published two companion pieces in *Philosophy Compass*, where they introduced the new label *conceptual ethics*, and pointed out that there had been a lot of debates in philosophy that engaged in the project of reflecting on what our terms and concepts in a certain realm should be (instead of focusing on the more traditional question of what our terms actually mean or what our ordinary concepts actually are). Haslanger's work on the amelioration of gender and race concepts was a central part of that literature, among others. More recently, Herman Cappelen (2018) wrote a monograph that attempted to give a systematic account of what ameliorating the meaning of terms or the content of concepts consists in (or, as he calls it, *conceptual engineering*). This literature has given rise to a growing interest in both ameliorative projects about a multitude of phenomena, and foundational questions about the prospects of amelioration. (In what follows, I will use the labels *amelioration*, *conceptual ethics*, and *conceptual engineering* interchangeably.)

Thus, the method of amelioration has had a huge influence on the philosophy of gender (and beyond), and many of the accounts that we will examine in this Element are inspired by this approach. However, parallelly, methodological reflections in mainstream metaphysics have often followed a different direction (see for instance Schaffer 2009 and Sider 2011), who have defended what Amie Thomasson (2015, 2017) calls *heavyweight metaphysical realism* about what metaphysical questions are about. In this Element, I am interested in exploring some of the methodological insights that can be learned from the metaphysics of gender. In my view, one of the virtues of recent debates on the metaphysics of gender is that they focus explicitly on methodological issues (as Haslanger 2000 beautifully exemplifies), and this is one of the ways in which the sub-field of the metaphysics of gender has had an impact on mainstream metaphysics. I will illustrate this influence by presenting and defending metaphysical deflationism, as a way of understanding how amelioration provides a method for metaphysics.[9]

---

[9] I do not mean to suggest that metaphysical deflationism is the only way of showing how amelioration is relevant for the metaphysics of gender. Indeed, Haslanger (2006, 2020) provides a different, more Quinean answer to this question (see Díaz-León forthcoming-b for further discussion of the differences). But metaphysical deflationism provides a very clear and systematic

First, I will examine Thomasson's alternative approach to meta-metaphysics. In particular, she develops and defends a version of *metaphysical deflationism*, which is an alternative to heavyweight realism. As we will see, a useful development of this view (and in particular, the direction that her more recent work has taken) has it that many questions in metaphysics are actually questions in conceptual ethics or conceptual engineering, that is, questions about what the central terms in a certain area should mean (or the concepts that they should express). I will then argue that we can use Thomasson's defence of metaphysical deflationism in order to justify the relevance of ameliorative projects in the metaphysics of gender. This will be the meta-metaphysical approach that I will undertake to explore in the second part of this Element. But before, I will need to assess some recent challenges to this kind of meta-metaphysical approach. In particular, I will examine some alternative approaches by Mikkola (2016), Dembroff (2018), Barnes (2020), Jenkins (2023), and, interestingly enough, Haslanger (2006) herself. I will assess whether these interesting perspectives pose an insurmountable challenge to the meta-metaphysical framework that I favour, and I will argue that they do not.

3 Thomasson's Defence of Metaphysical Deflationism

In this section I will explain the basic ideas behind Thomasson's defence of metaphysical deflationism, and in particular the version of the view that she has developed in her more recent work (e.g., 2017, 2020, 2021), where she argues that many debates in metaphysics are (or should be) ultimately about questions in conceptual engineering, that is, they are debates about what our terms in the

---

account of how amelioration is relevant for the metaphysics of gender, namely, by being the first step of the metaphysical inquiry. Other authors have developed different accounts of the meta-metaphysics of gender (and more generally, the meta-metaphysics of the social realm), such as Epstein (2015), Barnes (2014, 2017), Mikkola (2015, 2017), Griffith (2017, 2018), Schaffer (2017), Sider (2017), Passinsky (2021), Mason (2021), Richardson (2022, 2023), and Taylor (2023). In this Element I do not engage directly in discussion with all these alternative meta-metaphysical frameworks, since that would take us too far from questions about the metaphysics of gender. But I do contribute indirectly to this debate, by showing how an alternative framework, namely, metaphysical deflationism, can offer a useful account of what debates in the metaphysics of gender are about. This is not the only way of making sense of this question. Indeed, as feminist theorists have often taught us, exploring different frameworks and starting points is not always intended to answer the question of which framework is 'the right one', but how the different frameworks can offer illuminating and fruitful accounts of what the theories are about. It is in this spirit that I submit a defence of metaphysical deflationism as applied to gender. For further discussion see Díaz-León (2018) where I discuss Barnes (2014, 2017), and Díaz-León (2021) where I discuss Sider (2017). (In Díaz-León 2020a I drew from Mikkola 2015, whose account is similar in some central respects, such as allowing a role for normative considerations to be relevant in metaphysics, although as I understand her, Mikkola also shares Haslanger's Quinean assumptions.) I hope to discuss the other meta-metaphysical accounts more fully elsewhere. Thanks to an anonymous reviewer for pressing me on this.

relevant realm *should* mean (or the concepts they should express). Her first approach to this sort of view focused mostly on *existence questions* in metaphysics, that is, questions about whether different sorts of entities or kinds exist, or are really instantiated in the actual world, such as questions about whether medium-sized objects, numbers, propositions, consciousness, free will, and works of art really exist (Thomasson 2008). She was interested in the ordinary meaning of phrases such as 'X exists' or 'X is real'. As she explains:

> the truth-conditions for the object-language claim 'Ks don't exist' may be stated in the metalanguage: 'Ks don't exist' is true just in case the term 'K' doesn't refer – where the latter clearly does not require first referring to some object only to deny its existence. (2008: 65)

The idea here is that the truth conditions for a sentence of the form 'Ks don't exist' in the object-language we are interested in (which can be English, the same as the metalanguage we use to discuss the issue) are equivalent to the truth conditions for a sentence of the form '"K" doesn't refer'. This latter claim doesn't require that the term 'K' refers to a real thing in order for the sentence to be true. Clearly, the sentence can be true if that term in the object-language does not refer to anything. Hence, the truth-conditions for interesting claims such as 'Ks don't exist' (say 'numbers do not exist' or 'propositions do not exist') are clear enough: the philosophical debate about existence is reduced to questions about whether certain terms in the object-language (which can be identical to the meta-language) pick out entities in the actual world or not. From this idea, she argues, 'we can then get the following schema about existence: Ks exist if and only if 'K' refers'. (2008: 65)

This schema (what she calls schema (E)) is key to solving metaphysical debates about existence, since it shifts the focus from existence questions to questions about reference of central terms. How could schema (E) help to make progress in debates about the metaphysics of gender? Debates about the *existence* of gender are not as central to the metaphysics of gender as in other areas of metaphysics (e.g., numbers, medium-sized objects, or propositions), but they are pretty central in debates about the metaphysics of race (see for instance Appiah 1985, Glasgow 2009, and Hochman 2019, who all advocate for versions of anti-realism about race, and who follow an approach that is very congenial to Thomasson's approach, since they all focus on whether *racial terms* refer to real entities or not). However, it is easy to modify the approach so that it also applies to gender. Central questions in the metaphysics of gender have to do with the nature of gender (that is, what determines someone's gender, what it would take for someone to have a certain gender), and with questions about inclusion and exclusion, that is, what are the membership conditions for belonging to a certain gender, and who satisfies those membership conditions. It is easy to see how schema (E) could help us make progress with respect to these questions too: questions about the reference of a general term 'K' can help us make progress with respect to questions about the membership conditions for being a member of kind K. That is, questions about *what it would take* for someone to fall under term 'K' are relevant in order to make progress with respect to debates about the nature of kind K and about who belongs to kind K.

However, this sort of approach to metaphysical questions about gender (and in general) has received some resistance. Thomasson already considers a common objection and deals with it in a very compelling manner. She says:

> A . . . common objection is that this schema misrepresents existence claims as being about language, when they are really about the world and the things in it. But that is not so: on this view, existence claims are the object language correlates of reference claims, but involve a form of semantic descent from claims about reference to claims in the object language, using, rather than mentioning, the disputed terms. Since they use rather than mention the terms, existence claims themselves are of course about the world. The claim is not one of synonymy, but rather that schema (E) demonstrates a connection between the rules of use for our terms 'refer' and 'exist', which enables us to move up and down the semantic slide, from mentioning terms in discussing whether they refer, to using those terms in talking about whether or not entities of the sort exist. (2008: 66)

The central idea, as we can see, is that schema (E) does not entail that existence questions are just questions about language, and not about the way the world is. Existence questions are first-order questions in the object-language, that is, they are claims in the object-language that use some terms (rather than mentioning them) in order to say something about *what the world is like.* According to schema (E) these existence claims in the object-language are equivalent to (i.e., have the same truth-conditions as) reference claims in the meta-language. That is, we can move back and forth between claims in the object language that *use* some terms to say something about the world, to meta-linguistic claims in the metalanguage that *mention* the same terms to say something about what those terms refer to. And this is due to the conceptual connection between existence language and reference language.

Thomasson (2008) is mostly concerned with existence questions, but in her recent work she has further extended her approach with respect to other metaphysical questions. For instance, Thomasson (2012) says:

> Metaphysics is not only traditionally concerned with what exists . . . but also with questions about the *natures* of things of various sorts. Thus other important problems in metaphysics are questions about the natures, for

example, of persons, artifacts or works of art: what are their essential properties? What does it take for something to be a person, an artifact, or a work of
art? Are humans, or artifacts, or works of art, essentially tied to their
origins? ... All of these questions about natures, identity and persistence
conditions are modal questions: questions about the properties an object *must*
have to be of a certain type, about what it *would* take for there to be something
of a given type, about the conditions under which individuals would be
identical, or under which a given thing would or would not persist. Under
this heading also come questions not about whether something of a given sort
exists, but about what it *would* take for something of a given sort (or for an
individual) to exist: about the existence conditions for things of various kinds.
(2012: 15, my emphasis)

This develops the idea I mentioned earlier, to wit, that we can use schema (E) to
make progress not only with respect to existence questions of the form 'Do Ks
exist?', but also with respect to other metaphysical questions of the form 'What
would it take for Ks to exist?'[10] Namely, we can figure out the conditions for Ks
to *exist*, by means of figuring out the conditions for term 'K' to *refer*. If we can
figure out what it takes for our term 'K' to refer to certain individuals, then we
can make a lot of progress with respect to metaphysical questions about the
nature of kind K. In particular, in Thomasson's view, we need to figure out the
application conditions for the term 'K', that is, what it would take for someone
to fall under the term 'K', that is, to belong to kind K. Hence, there is a strong
conceptual connection between the application conditions for term 'K', and the
membership conditions for kind K. A natural consequence of schema (E) is the
following:

X is a member of kind K iff X falls under the term 'K'.

Hence, on Thomasson's approach, to figure out the application conditions for
a term 'K' will be illuminating with respect to the membership conditions for
kind K, which in turn will be illuminating with respect to the nature of kind K.[11]
In Thomasson's view, in order to figure out whether an individual falls under
term 'K' (and hence belongs to kind K), we need to go through *two* different steps.
In the first step, we need to figure out the *application conditions* for term 'K'. The
application conditions, in Thomasson's view, amount to the information about the

---

[10] Here we are mostly interested in expressions that belong to the category of general terms or
predicates, that is, terms that apply to a class of things, such as 'water', 'tiger', or 'chair'. In the
case of debates about gender, we are concerned with the term 'gender' in general, as well as
specific gender categories such as 'man', 'woman', and 'genderqueer'. In this case, these terms
are supposed to refer to human kinds.

[11] But see further for a further clarification: the application conditions can sometimes only say what
it would take for a kind to be the referent of the general term, not which kind is the actual referent.
More on this further.

rules of use of term 'K' that are grasped when competent speakers grasp the meaning of the term. This information is not very rich in the case of many general terms, especially in the case of natural kind terms, since we can be competent users of the terms without having substantive knowledge about the membership conditions of the term. However, Thomasson argues, when we are competent users of a term, we have at least some information that allows us to *anchor* the term to the world. This is part of what it takes for members of a linguistic community to successfully refer to a kind K (to refer to Ks) by employing their term 'K'. As Thomasson puts it: 'our terms must at least have very basic grounding conditions, establishing what it takes for the term to acquire reference at all' (2008: 68). And she adds:

> Though these may only involve (e.g.) an open list of sufficient conditions for application of the term, rather than a set of necessary and sufficient conditions, they may still be useful in evaluating existence claims. So, e.g., supposing it is sufficient for the term 'law' to apply that the members of the legislature vote for a bill which the president signs, we can infer that the term refers and so that there is a law if those conditions are fulfilled. (2008: 69)

Thomasson's view (which she first presented in 2008 and later developed in 2012, 2015, 2017, 2020, and elsewhere) is that even if it is true that for many terms, competent speakers do not necessarily know a set of necessary and sufficient conditions for something to fall under the term, competent speakers often have some information that can be useful in order to evaluate existence claims. For instance, competent users of the term 'law' would agree with the following conditional: 'If the members of the legislature have voted for a bill X which the president signs, then X is a law.' This conditional gives sufficient conditions for X to fall under the term 'law', and therefore, this sort of knowledge would help us evaluate existence claims concerning laws. In particular, we can know that if the antecedent is satisfied, the consequent will be satisfied and at least some laws exist.

On this modest view, for some other terms we might not know sufficient conditions (or at least not substantive enough to allow us to evaluate existence claims), but we might know *necessary* conditions instead. That is, for some terms, competent speakers associate the terms with some *sortal* information about the kind of thing the referents are. For instance, we all know that tigers are animals, that water is a liquid (at room temperature) and that women are human. These minimal necessary conditions also allow us to evaluate some metaphysical claims, since we can infer that if an individual does not satisfy those necessary conditions, then they cannot be a member of the corresponding kind.

But do we really associate application conditions of this sort, as either necessary or sufficient conditions for something to fall under the term, with our general terms, when we grasp their meaning? Didn't Kripke (1972) and Putnam (1973) already teach us that meanings are not in our heads, that is, that grasping the meaning of a general term does not consist in having identifying knowledge of the referent? But in Thomasson's view, application conditions are weaker than identifying knowledge. They are not in the form of necessary and sufficient conditions. They might merely amount to either some necessary conditions, or some sufficient conditions (often pretty trivial). However, this already helps us to make some progress when evaluating existence claims. As Thomasson explains:

> The fact that competent speakers typically cannot state application conditions for most of the terms they use is no evidence at all against the idea that our terms have application conditions. Application conditions should be thought of as semantic rules analogous to grammatical rules . . . rather than thinking of application conditions as definitions competent speakers (or anyone else) could recite, we should instead think of them as rules for when it is and is not proper to use a term, which speakers master in acquiring competence with applying and refusing a new term in various situations, and that (once mastered) enable competent speakers to evaluate whether or not the term would properly be applied in a range of actual and hypothetical situations. If we think of application conditions this way, we can after all hope to gain help in evaluating existence claims via claims about reference, and those about reference via appeal to application conditions. (2008: 69–70)

The idea, then, is that knowledge of application conditions is rather implicit, and difficult to make explicit in the form of explicit definitions. On the contrary, it amounts to our dispositions to apply the term to different individuals in different situations in different scenarios. These are the raw materials from which the theoretical notion of 'application conditions' is coined, but this is nothing over and above our raw dispositions to apply the term in different situations given different fully described scenarios.

As I said earlier, figuring out the application conditions for a term 'K' is the first step of a two-step process in order to find out whether an individual X falls under term 'K'. This first step is *conceptual*: it amounts to making explicit the implicit knowledge of application conditions we already had. In her early work, Thomasson referred to this step as *conceptual analysis*, or analysis of ordinary concepts (e.g., 2008, 2012) whereas in her more recent work, she is moving towards the view that this step involves substantive work in *conceptual engineering*, that is, *normative* conceptual work (2016, 2020, 2021). On the other hand, the second step of the metaphysical inquiry is *empirical*: it amounts to finding out whether the corresponding individuals satisfy the relevant application conditions that we identified in step 1. This can only be figured out empirically. Hence, ontological claims such as 'Ks exist' or 'Bs are Ks' can only be figured out empirically, since the crucial second step of figuring out whether some individuals at all (or Bs more particularly) happen to satisfy the application conditions for term 'K' we identified in the first step can only be discovered empirically.[12] Thomasson (2015) calls this two-step process in order to evaluate ontological claims 'easy ontology', since on this view debates in ontology can be reduced to questions in conceptual analysis and empirical work, with no additional need for deep metaphysical knowledge (that cannot be reduced to either conceptual or empirical work). This view is in contrast with what she calls 'heavyweight realism' about metaphysics, according to which debates in metaphysics are to be solved by means of sui generis epistemic methods that supposedly give us special access to metaphysical truths. One of the virtues of Thomasson's meta-metaphysical framework is that it makes our access to metaphysical truths much less mysterious, since conceptual work and empirical work are familiar epistemic methods. However, as Thomasson herself has recently acknowledged (e.g., Thomasson 2016, 2020), purely descriptive conceptual analysis alone cannot help us make progress in many debates in metaphysics. One reason is that conceptual analysis is methodologically problematic as well. It is not clear whether our semantic intuitions give us good reasons to posit alleged conceptual truths. Moreover, as a matter of fact, there seems to be a lot of divergence regarding people's semantic intuitions and what they consider to be conceptually true. This is connected with the well-known problem of *ignorance and error* for *descriptivist* theories of meaning for general terms, which goes as follows. According to descriptivist views, the meaning of general terms is given by the descriptions we associate with the terms, or at least the *inferential dispositions* we have involving those terms (such as the fact that we are disposed to infer 'x is bachelor' from the belief 'x is an unmarried man'). However, this view faces the well-known problem of ignorance and error, to wit: On the one hand, many or most competent speakers of a given general term can be massively mistaken about the features of the referents of the term, but they still successfully refer to the kind that they share (that is to say, associating certain descriptions with a term 'K' that is uniquely satisfied by a kind is not *sufficient* to refer to it). On the other hand, many or most competent users of the term 'K' can be ignorant of any identifying descriptions, but they still

---

[12] The two-step process is also defended by Chalmers and Jackson (2001) as well as in Chalmers (1996) and Jackson (1998).

successfully refer to kind K (that is to say, associating identifying descriptions with a term that is satisfied by a kind K is not *necessary* to refer to K).[13]

As we saw earlier, Thomasson's response to this sort of worry is that the application conditions associated with a term do not have to be in the form of necessary and sufficient conditions. Rather, they can be pretty minimal, in the form of only necessary or only sufficient conditions. However, it is not clear that even this weaker criterion is met often. For many of our concepts, it is not clear that all competent speakers share a unique set of application conditions. There is a lot of divergence among different speakers. Also, it is not clear how we can ascertain the application conditions that we actually associate with our terms. As Thomasson explains, this is implicit knowledge that is often very difficult to make explicit. But do we really have reliable methods to make it explicit? In addition, in many cases there seems to be indeterminacy as to what the application conditions are, or what kind they would pick out. Given all these reasons (divergence, error, ignorance, and indeterminacy), the prospects of conceptual analysis (in the sense of descriptive analysis of our ordinary concepts) are not good.

However, more recently, Thomasson has defended the view that the first step of the easy ontology methodology can and often does involve a lot of normative work regarding what concept we *should* use rather than what concept we actually use. According to Thomasson (2016, 2020) many traditional debates in metaphysics already involved a lot of revisionary claims on the basis of normative conceptual work. Hence, many metaphysical theses that were supposed to be about our *ordinary* concepts should be seen as claims about the concepts that we *should* employ, or the meaning that some central terms should have.

This renewed meta-metaphysical framework is very congenial with Haslanger's tripartite distinction of three different approaches to philosophical questions of the form 'what is X?', and in particular with her emphasis on ameliorative projects. This is the meta-metaphysical framework that I aim to explore in the rest of this Element, as applied to the metaphysics of gender.

However, many feminist metaphysicians are sceptical that this sort of framework can be useful in order to make progress in the metaphysics of gender. In the next section, I will assess some of the central challenges to the ameliorative approach to metaphysics that I wish to explore, and I will argue that they do not pose unsurmountable challenges. In particular, as we will see, these challenges have the form of pointing towards some concerns that feminist metaphysics should pay attention to. I will argue that metaphysical deflationism is compatible with those concerns.

---

[13] See Devitt and Sterelny (1999) for a very useful discussion of the ignorance and error argument.

4 Are Debates in the Metaphysics of Gender about Which Concepts We Should Use?

4.1 Barnes on the Connection between the Metaphysics of Gender and the Meaning of Gender Terms

Elizabeth Barnes (2020) has posed an interesting challenge to the kind of meta-metaphysical framework I wish to defend. She argues that in order to make progress in the metaphysics of gender, it is not useful to focus on giving accounts of the truth-conditions of sentences involving gender terms such as 'man' and 'woman'. But this seems to be in tension with Thomasson's framework, and in particular with schema (E) earlier. As I said, on this view, in order to evaluate ontological claims about the nature and existence of a certain kind K, it is a useful first step to examine the application conditions for term 'K', in order to know what it would take for 'K' to refer, and whether those conditions are actually satisfied in the world. But Barnes (2020) says:

> Philosophical theories of gender are typically understood as theories of what it is to be a woman, a man, a nonbinary person, and so on. In this paper, I argue that this is a mistake. There's good reason to suppose that our best philosophical theory of gender might not directly match up to or give the extensions of ordinary gender categories like 'woman'. ... The project of developing a philosophical theory of gender can and should come apart from the project of giving definitions or truth conditions for sentences involving our gender terms. (2020: 704)

Why does Barnes think that in order to develop a theory of gender, we should not engage in the project of giving application conditions for gender terms, *contra* Thomasson? The main reason, as I understand it, is that in Barnes' view, it is possible that the social structures that underlie our gender practices and give rise to gender categories do not correspond to neat metaphysical categories such as 'manhood' and 'womanhood'. That is to say, the metaphysics of social reality might not contain gender categories such as 'man' and 'woman'. In her view, the best explanation of our gendered social practices might not invoke metaphysical categories that correspond to our terms 'man' and 'woman'. It might be the case that the truth conditions for our sentences involving gender terms such as 'man' and 'woman' do not really match up with the underlying gender categories that better explain social reality.

As Barnes puts it:

> Rather, giving a metaphysics of gender should be understood as the project of theorizing what it is – if anything – about the social world that ultimately explains gender. But that project might come apart from the project of defining or giving application conditions for our natural language gender terms like 'woman'. (706)

This gives rise to the question: In what cases would the project of giving application conditions for *gender terms*, and the project of theorizing the nature of *gender*, come apart? Barnes (2020) suggests three different reasons, as I understand her view. As a first approach, the three reasons are as follows: (i) gender terms might refer to different things in different contexts, (ii) the basic social structures explaining our gendered social practices might not correspond to the meaning of gender terms such as 'man' and 'woman', and (iii) we might have ameliorative reasons for using gender terms such as 'man' and 'woman' in ways that depart from what those terms actually pick out. As a first response to each reason (I will elaborate these responses next): against (i) I would say that this point is compatible with Thomasson's framework. If the term refers to different kinds in different contexts, then the two-step process has to be applied in each context, yielding different answers. Nothing in Thomasson's view requires that a given term refers to the same kind in all contexts. In response to (ii), I would say that even if we can usefully distinguish between the reference of our gender terms such as 'man' and 'woman', and the bedrock social categories that explain our gendered social practices, this does not mean that the application conditions for gender terms are irrelevant in metaphysics. In particular, in order to figure out those bedrock social categories, it is indispensable that we figure out the application conditions of gender terms, and the connection between the actual referents of gender terms, and those bedrock social categories. There are different metaphysical views here: gender categories (i.e., the referents of gender terms) might be constituted by, or grounded in, those bedrock social categories. Or perhaps the metaphysical connection is weaker than that: maybe there is a mere causal connection. However, if those bedrock social categories are to explain our gendered social practices, we need to figure out the metaphysical connections between those social categories and our gender categories. And for this inquiry, figuring out the application conditions of gender terms is an indispensable first step. Furthermore, in response to (iii), I would say that this is a good point, but very similar to Haslanger's ameliorative project. Indeed, we need to distinguish between what gender terms *actually* refer to, and what gender terms *should* refer to (perhaps in different contexts), but Haslanger (2000) already taught us this. This is compatible with Thomasson's conceptual engineering version of her deflationist view.

Let's examine in more detail Barnes' objections. She says:

> I do think people can be systematically wrong about gender. Moreover, I think that a theory of what gender really is ought to be able to influence how gender terms are used. It might not be surprising if our metaphysics of material objects doesn't give us might guidance for how to use a word like 'table', but we want our metaphysics of gender to have at least some relevance to how we use words like 'woman'. (713)

She suggests in this passage that the metaphysics of material objects like tables might come apart from theories about the application conditions of 'table'. This is in tension with Thomasson's approach earlier, and in particular with schema (E). However, Barnes does acknowledge that in the case of gender, we do want the metaphysics of gender to say something about our use of gender terms. But she adds: 'on the best interpretation of social position accounts of gender, they shouldn't be thought of as giving us a metaphysical analysis of what it is to be a man or a woman, or of giving us straightforward application conditions for gender terms like "man" and "woman"' (714). By social position accounts of gender, she refers to accounts along the lines of Haslanger's ameliorative account of gender in terms of someone's social position in a social hierarchy, as I explained earlier. Here again Barnes emphasizes the idea that the metaphysics of gender, and analyses of the application conditions of gender terms, can come apart, *contra* meta-metaphysical views like Thomasson's. What are Barnes' reasons for this claim? She says:

> Saying that the social structure of masculinization and feminization is the ultimate metaphysical explanation of gender, however, needn't imply that it's the full story about gender, as Haslanger herself acknowledges. Gender also encompasses gender identity, gender expression, and so on. And of course these things all matter greatly to our experience of gender, and saying that social position is the full or complete account of gender would be far too reductive. But a social position metaphysics allows us to say that these further components of gender can ultimately be explained in terms of the basic binary social structure that attributes social significance to perceived biological sex, and which privileges some and disadvantages others based on assumptions about what ought to follow from being perceived as male or female. (715)

This passage contains the core idea behind Barnes' argument, as I understand it. First, she claims that gender is not one thing but many things. Second, she suggests that whereas there are certain bedrocks social categories that offer the best explanation of gendered social practices (namely, Haslangerian social structures), the metaphysics of gender is not exhausted by them. There is more to gender than those bedrock social categories, although these social categories offer the best explanation of gendered social practices and hence the metaphysics of gender should point that out. But at the same time, it seems likely that our gender terms do not currently pick out exactly those bedrock social categories. And indeed, focusing on what gender terms *should* pick out, it might not correspond to those bedrock social categories either, but rather, say, to gender self-identification. Hence, Barnes argues, the metaphysics of gender is ultimately about those bedrock social categories, but our gender terms might not (nor should they) pick out those bedrock social categories. Hence, the metaphysics of gender comes apart from the meaning of gender terms.

In response: this last inference is too quick. I agree that it is useful to think about the bedrock social categories that could offer the best explanation of our gendered social practices, and that they might come apart from either the descriptive meaning or the ameliorative meaning of gender terms. But this does not entail that our two-step process as described by Thomasson is irrelevant. Indeed, I believe it is indispensable. The reason is that in order to figure out what the bedrock social categories underlying gendered practices are, we cannot do without analysing the meaning of gender terms. As I suggested earlier, if those bedrock social categories provide the best explanation of our gendered social practices, this might be due to either a *constitutive* relation or a *causal* relation between those bedrock social categories and gender categories such as 'man', 'woman', and 'genderqueer'. And, crucially, in order to ascertain which relation holds, we need to engage in the two-step process a la Thomasson. For we need to figure out what our current (or revisionary) gender categories are, in order to figure out what are the bedrock social practices that better explain our gender categories. That is, we need to know what our gender terms pick out (or should pick out), in order to figure out what bedrock social categories either constitute or causally explain our current (or revisionary) gender categories. It is not clear to me how we could figure out what bedrock gender categories could better explain our gendered social practices if we do not know what our current gender categories are. Or alternatively, in case the *descriptive* question was too indeterminate to figure out, we should at least figure out what our *revisionary* gender categories should be, and what bedrock social categories better explain them.

Barnes adds:

> On this view, there is a bedrock social structure that gives rise to the complicated, multi-faceted social experience of gender. When doing the metaphysics of gender, this basic social structure is something it makes sense to focus on. But it would be overly reductive to say that such a social structure is what gender is, or what gives us the extension of our gender terms. Gender is many, complicated things – but many, complicated things which are ultimately explained by a hierarchical social structure. (717)

This is compatible with the idea I just sketched. Even if Barnes is right (as I am sympathetic to) that there are bedrock social categories (a la Haslanger) that explain our gendered social practices, there are still many kinds in the vicinity of gender, and hence our gender terms probably do not (and *should not*) pick out only those bedrock social categories. I completely agree. But as I have argued, this does not rule out the relevance of Thomasson's two-step inquiry. On the contrary, this only calls out for a *context-sensitive* application of the two-step inquiry.

4.2 Dembroff on the 'Real Talk' Assumption about Gender

In this section I will examine another interesting challenge to the version of metaphysical deflationism I am advocating. Dembroff (2018) has argued that it is a mistake to try to account for the nature of gender by assuming what they call the 'Real Gender' assumption. This is, roughly, the idea that we should use gender terms in a way that closely matches gender kind membership facts, that is to say, facts about who belongs to which gender. This assumption, Dembroff argues, is common both in anti-feminist critique and in feminist arguments. As Dembroff puts it:

> This manifestation seems to rely on the idea that gender classifications should track the gender kind membership facts. Call this the 'Real Gender' assumption. According to this assumption, someone should be classified as a man only if they 'really are' a man – that is, only if man is a recognized gender, and they meet its membership conditions. (2018: 22)

Dembroff claims that many feminist scholars also make this assumption, since they aim to give accounts of how we should use gender terms (and what should guide our gender classifications, which are linguistic practices) in terms of the real gender facts, that is, in terms of the real nature of underlying gender kinds. Gender classifications include gender terms such as 'man', 'woman', and 'genderqueer', as well as other gendered expressions such as pronouns and other gender markers in our natural languages. Dembroff claims that this assumption is common both in those anti-trans discourses that attempt to argue that gender terms should track facts about biological sex because these are the real membership conditions for the operative gender kinds, and in the work of feminist philosophers that aim to defend the opposite view. For instance, Dembroff mentions Mari Mikkola as a trans-inclusive feminist philosopher who also makes the 'Real Gender' assumption:

> Mikkola suggests that we prefer theories of gender that align with certain political commitments regarding gender classification. Trans identities deserve to be respected in our classifications, so theories of gender should be sensitive to these identities and avoid implying that trans identities do not track the relevant gender kinds. But here again, we find the Real Gender assumption. Without this assumption, it is unclear why we should ensure that theories of gender align with what we take to be just gender classification practices. Ontological oppression exposes the flaw with the Real Gender assumption: it presupposes that the gender kinds operating in one's context are not deeply distorted and unjust. This presupposition is not justified. (2018: 32)

Dembroff' central idea is that the methodological assumption to the effect that metaphysicians should offer metaphysical accounts of the nature of gender that track what we take to be just gender classifications, is not justified. The main reason is that it might be the case that the metaphysical nature of gender kinds does not actually match up with what we take to be just gender classifications, because it might be the case that the nature of the operative gender kinds is oppressive, and hence does not match up with just gender classifications. Dembroff puts the core argument as follows:

1. The Real Gender assumption should not guide gender classifications in contexts where the operative gender kinds are oppressive.
2. Dominant gender kinds oppress trans and nonbinary persons.
3. So, the Real Gender assumption should not guide gender classifications in dominant contexts.

In dominant contexts, it is wrongheaded to determine gender classifications by looking to operative gender kinds. But how, then, should they be decided? What should guide gender classifications? (2018: 35–6)

Dembroff's main argument for premise 2 goes as follows: 'dominant gender kinds systematically oppress persons who claim trans and non-binary identities. They do not reveal what gender classification practices should be; they reveal what these practices have been' (2018: 35). As we can see, Dembroff's central idea is that since dominant gender kinds systematically oppress people who do not fall under binary gender categories, then these dominant gender kinds cannot be a guide for our gender classifications, since if we base our gender classifications on the operative gender kinds in our vicinity, then our gender classifications will be oppressive since the underlying gender kind membership facts are oppressive. And the other way around: if we try to investigate the nature of operative gender kinds based on what we take to be just gender classifications, as Mikkola suggests (on Dembroff's interpretation), then we will not get a justified account of the metaphysics of gender kinds, since we are assuming that operative gender kinds track just gender classifications, but this might not be true. And given the oppressive nature of operative gender kinds, it is likely that this assumption will be false.

Dembroff's argument is useful and illuminating, and it is especially interesting for our purposes since it seems to be in tension with the meta-metaphysical framework I have been advocating so far. In particular, Dembroff seems to suggest that we should not investigate the nature of gender kinds on the basis of what we take to be just gender classifications. But on the two-step metaphysical inquiry that I have been defending, that is exactly what the metaphysician of gender should do. The first step is a project in conceptual engineering where we investigate the application conditions that gender terms should have, and then we are in a position to undertake the second step where we investigate empirically what individuals if any satisfy those application conditions (and therefore belong to the corresponding kind).

In other words: from Thomasson's schema (E) earlier it follows that a term 'K' refers only if Ks exist. This seems to suggest that a term 'K' refers to a group of individuals only if that group of individuals instantiate the property of being K. Applied to gender, this in turn seems to entail something like the 'Real Gender' assumption, to wit: someone should be classified as falling under the term 'K' only if they belong to kind K, that is, if they meet the membership conditions.

In response, I want to argue that metaphysical deflationism, and in particular schema (E) earlier, do not entail the 'Real Gender' assumption in a problematic way. There are several reasons for this. The first reason is that the 'Real Gender' assumption, as Dembroff puts it, is about what our gender classifications *should* be like. The 'Real Gender' assumption has it that our gender classifications should be guided by the membership facts of the *dominant* gender kinds. And this is clearly false, for the reasons Haslanger (2000) already made clear: there might be good ameliorative reasons for why the dominant gender kinds are not the *best referents* for our gender terms, that is, the referents that gender terms should have (even if they are the referents they actually have). When we engage in the *ameliorative* project, we might have good reasons to revise the meaning of our gender terms and change the referents, so that they do no longer refer to the operative gender kinds in the vicinity, but to new gender kinds so to speak. It is clear that Haslanger's ameliorative project is not committed to the 'Real Gender' assumption: Haslanger's ameliorative project is not interested in describing the meaning of gender terms on the basis of the referents that they actually have (the dominant gender kinds), but in terms of the referents that they *should* have (that is, what we can call *ameliorative gender kinds*).

However (and this is my second critique of Dembroff's argument), once we change the meaning of gender terms given our best ameliorative reasons, we are then in a good position to investigate the metaphysics of gender, that is, the nature of these new gender kinds. The metaphysics of gender is not only about what dominant gender kinds are like (which are oppressive as Dembroff shows), but also about what less oppressive, more liberating gender kinds could be like. This is also the business of the metaphysics of gender. Dembroff's argument assumes that the metaphysics of gender is only about the nature of dominant gender kinds. But as Talia Bettcher (2009) already suggested, we can distinguish between different gender claims. Bettcher (2009) distinguished between *dominant* gender meanings that are common in mainstream communities, and *resistant* gender meanings that are operative in trans-friendly communities. The former are not inclusive of trans people, but the latter are. Bettcher (2009) focuses on the *meaning* of gender terms, but in my view, her argument also extends to the nature of gender *kinds*. The two different patterns of use of gender terms that Bettcher (2009) identifies give rise to two different sorts of gender facts. On the other hand, there are dominant gender kinds that have membership conditions that are oppressive for trans and non-binary people. On the other hand, there are resistant gender kinds that are trans-inclusive. An exhaustive theory of the metaphysics of gender should invoke all these kinds.

Hence, there are two ways in which schema (E) earlier *does not* entail the 'Real Gender' assumption. Firstly, even if it is true that term 'K' refers to Ks, and in particular, given the application conditions that term 'K' actually has, it follows that certain individuals (and not others) are Ks, it does not follow that we *should* say that those and only those are Ks. The fact that something is true does not entail that we *should say* it. There are truths that are such that should remain unsaid. This does not entail that we should utter the negation of those truths. Rather, it might be the case that we should just stay silent on the matter. Secondly, as I have suggested, it might be the case that even if 'K' actually refers to Ks given the ordinary meaning of 'K', we *ought* to change the meaning of term 'K' for ameliorative reasons, so that it comes to have a different referent. And once the term 'K' acquires the new referent, 'K' does no longer refer to Ks, but to a new group, K*s, so there is no longer a reason to say of those Ks that they fall under 'K', as the real gender assumption would have it, because this would be no longer true. That is, now the term 'K' refers to K*s, not Ks.

What are the consequences of this discussion with respect to the two-step method that I have advocated, following Thomasson? It is clear that Dembroff's arguments do not pose an obstacle to our meta-metaphysical framework. We have to be aware of the distinction between the gender kinds that match up with ordinary gender concepts, which might be oppressive gender kinds, since our ordinary gender concepts are probably not just, and the gender kinds that match up with the revisionary meaning of gender terms, that is, the meaning that gender terms should have, given ameliorative reasons. But this is not new: Haslanger (2000) already made this very clear. However, the reminder is always useful.

On the meta-metaphysical framework I have advocated, we should investigate the nature of gender kinds by means of examining first the application conditions of our gender terms. But as I have already emphasized (and as Thomasson has emphasized in her recent work), the interesting project is not only to figure out what our ordinary gender concepts refer to, but crucially, what our revisionary gender concepts should refer to. This is why the first step in the two-step process is a project in conceptual engineering, not descriptive conceptual analysis, as I have painstakingly argued, drawing both on Thomasson's and Haslanger's work.

However, for some purposes, we might be interested in examining the nature of dominant gender kinds and the ways in which they are oppressive. For these purposes, then, Dembroff is right that we cannot base our metaphysical inquiry merely in the study of *just* gender classifications, because dominant gender kinds might not match (and probably will not match) just gender classifications. For this purpose, we need to investigate first the application conditions of ordinary gender concepts, and then figure out the dominant gender kinds that they refer to. But as I have argued, the metaphysics of gender is not limited to this descriptive project. The metaphysics of gender (and many other projects in metaphysics, on Thomasson's approach) is not only about the kinds that our terms actually pick out, but also, and more crucially, about the kinds that our terms should pick out.

In addition, we can also see that we are not committed to the 'Real Gender' assumption in the other direction of the principle that Dembroff was also worried about. In particular, we are not assuming that our gender terms should always track the operative gender kinds in the vicinity, whatever they are. As I have explained, and as Haslanger (2000) already made clear, it might be the case that the actual referents of our gender terms are oppressive, and that we have good reasons to change their meaning.

To conclude our discussion so far: when it comes to claims about what should guide our gender classifications, this is clearly an ameliorative question about the meaning that our gender terms should have. Dembroff (2018) is obviously right that the usage of gender terms should not be constrained by the dominant gender-kind membership facts, because these gender kinds might be oppressive (and probably will be). The meaning that gender terms should have probably departs from the meaning that gender terms actually have. On the other hand, it is not true that the metaphysics of gender is only about the dominant gender kinds in our vicinity. This is an important aspect, but not the only one. With respect to the project of investigating the nature of dominant gender kinds, it is true we cannot be guided by just gender classifications, since there might be a mismatch. We should investigate the application conditions of ordinary gender concepts in order to ascertain what gender kinds they actually track, and how they are oppressive. Moreover, we should also investigate the application conditions that our gender terms *should* have, that is, those that are more conducive to social justice, and the corresponding gender kinds that they should track. The metaphysics of gender is also concerned with investigating the nature of these ameliorative gender kinds that our gender terms do not actually track but should track. And in order to figure this out, our two-step process is indispensable.

4.3 Further Objections to the Role of Application Conditions

According to the proposed methodological approach, we need to engage in the two-step inquiry as advocated by Thomasson. But an important clarification is in order. Firstly, as I have said, in many cases in the first step we will not be able to provide full accounts in terms of necessary and sufficient conditions for someone to fall under the concept (in this sense I agree with Mikkola). In many cases, partial analyses in terms of either necessary or sufficient conditions will be all we can achieve. But secondly, and more crucially, these accounts in terms of either necessary or sufficient conditions are still not accounts of the *membership conditions*, that is, the conditions that determine whether someone falls under the concept or belongs to the corresponding kind. This is the business of the second (empirical) step, not the first (conceptual) step. Let me explain in more detail.

As I said earlier, the first (conceptual) step is concerned with providing necessary and/or sufficient conditions regarding *what it would take* for something or someone to fall under the concept. What does this mean? Let's use an example. In the case of many natural kind terms such as 'water' or 'tiger', the first step can only deliver information about what it *would take for something* to fall under the concept, in a given scenario. In particular, we know that for something to fall under 'water', it would have to be watery stuff (that is, the odourless, colourless liquid that falls from the sky and fills rivers and lakes). But this does not mean that for a liquid sample to be water, it is necessary and sufficient that it is watery stuff. As is well known, something can be watery stuff and not be water (and vice versa). What is going on? The answer, as explained by Chalmers & Jackson (2001), is that the first step of the inquiry can only deliver *application conditions* regarding *what it would take* for something to fall under the concept, not *membership conditions*. Let me elaborate: application conditions are necessary and/or sufficient conditions for something (a feature, a property, a kind) to fall under the general term, given different scenarios, but these are not yet membership conditions for the corresponding kind *in the actual world*. The membership conditions for the kind are discovered by means of the second, empirical step, where we discover empirically what kinds or features, if any, satisfy those application conditions in the actual world. For example, going back to the case of 'water', in the first (conceptual) step we can discover that for something to fall under 'water' (in a fully described scenario), it has to be watery stuff. That is, we would apply the term 'water' in a possible scenario (where do not know what the watery stuff in front of us is made of) to a certain sample of liquid only if this is watery stuff. And once we figure out which stuff in our actual world is watery stuff, we can then apply the second step, by investigating empirically the nature of the (actual) watery stuff in front of us. That is, we can discover empirically that watery stuff in our vicinity is made of H_2O. (But if we had been born and raised in Twin Earth, we would then have discovered that the watery stuff in front of us is made of XYZ instead.) Hence, the application conditions for the concept 'water' amount to something like *being watery stuff*. But the membership conditions for X to be water (in the actual world) is that X is H_2O. Hence, the application conditions themselves cannot tell us what the nature of the (actual) referent is like. We need to engage in the second (empirical) step for that result. This is so especially in the case of terms that are *rigid designators*, like 'water' and 'tiger', that is to say, terms that refer to *the same property* or kind in all possible worlds where they refer at all. For this reason, there could be possible worlds where water (that is, H_2O) is not watery stuff. Thus, only by means of investigating empirically the nature of what happens to be watery stuff in our vicinity can we learn what the nature of water is like. However, for other terms that are not *rigid designators*, like 'triangle', and others (more controversially) such as 'friend', 'chair' and 'dancing', the application conditions and the membership conditions can coincide. (In what follows I will put aside this complication unless it is relevant for the argument.)

Another objection to the idea that we need to provide accounts of the application conditions of gender terms in order to provide accounts of the metaphysics of gender has been presented by Mikkola (2016). She argues that feminist metaphysicians do not need to offer substantive accounts of the application conditions of gender terms. In particular, she argues that we do not need to provide substantive accounts of the meaning of gender expressions in terms of necessary and sufficient conditions. She argues that participants in the debate can rely on their *extensional intuitions* about gender terms, and that this suffices for the purposes of feminist metaphysics. She suggests that given the serious difficulties facing the project of giving an account in terms of necessary and sufficient conditions for the application of gender terms, we can make methodological progress by means of relying only on extensional intuitions, about which there is not so much disagreement. In response: Mikkola is right that it is extremely difficult to offer an account in terms of the necessary and sufficient conditions for someone to fall under a certain gender concept. There will be a lot of disagreement about what the necessary and sufficient conditions would be. But as we saw earlier, according to Thomasson (2008), even if it is the case that competent speakers do not usually have explicit knowledge about the necessary and sufficient conditions for someone to fall under a certain concept, competent speakers do often have some implicit knowledge, at least partial. And it is possible, in Thomasson's view, to make this implicit knowledge explicit, by means of philosophical reasoning, analysis of thought experiments, and so on. However, Mikkola would reply that in the case of gender concepts, a consensus is not forthcoming given the recalcitrance of the disagreements. I agree that in the case of gender, disagreements about the application conditions of gender concepts are especially recalcitrant. But as Thomasson (2008) explains, we often do not need to give full accounts of a concept in terms of necessary and sufficient conditions for someone to fall under the concept, in order to obtain interesting metaphysical conclusions. In particular, as we saw earlier, sometimes we can provide partial application conditions in terms of either some sufficient conditions for someone to fall under the concept, or some necessary conditions for someone to fall under the concept, and these partial analyses are sufficient to draw interesting metaphysical conclusions. For example, from the claim that it is sufficient that X is P, for X to be G, we can conclude that given that we have empirical evidence that some individuals instantiate property P, we can infer that those individuals are G and hence Gs exist. Likewise, from the claim that it is necessary for X to be G that X is P, we can conclude that some individuals who clearly lack feature P, are clearly not Gs. Hence, partial analyses are sufficient for substantive metaphysical claims.

However, Mikkola could respond that in the case of gender concepts, even partial analyses in terms of either sufficient conditions or necessary conditions for someone to fall under the concepts will be difficult to agree upon. In response, I believe that *extensional* intuitions will probably also be very difficult to agree upon. Extensional intuitions are supposed to be intuitions about the individuals who actually fall under gender concepts. These intuitions are supposed to be neutral regarding what features are necessary and sufficient for someone to fall under the concept. Mikkola's claim is that whereas many participants in the debate about gender disagree about the necessary and sufficient conditions for someone to fall under a gender concept, most of those participants would agree about paradigmatic cases of individuals who do fall under the concept. For instance, everyone would agree that Madonna, Beyoncé, and Hillary Clinton are all women. Mikkola argues that relying on extensional intuitions like those is sufficient to explain our usage of the term 'woman', since we can all use the term competently even if we are not able to spell out necessary and sufficient conditions for someone to fall under the term. In response, I believe that even if there could be agreement about some non-controversial paradigmatic cases, there will probably be a lot of disagreement about who belongs and who does not belong to the extension of gender terms. That is, our extensional intuitions are also subject to disagreement. Extensional intuitions can vary a lot between different speakers and different communities. For instance, when it comes to contested cases, for example, whether trans women are women, unfortunately there is no agreement, and many people believe that (at least some) trans women do not fall under the concept 'woman'.[14] Even if we focus on the more modest question of who can be posited as paradigmatic individuals, there will be disagreement. As Bettcher (2009) argues, when it comes to analysing the meaning of 'woman', some theorists will want to start from paradigmatic instances that do not include trans women, but this is problematic in her view, for both *descriptive* and *normative* reasons. That is, it is wrong for descriptive reasons since there are speakers who do include trans women as paradigms (e.g., members of trans-friendly communities). And, secondly, because it could be argued, following Bettcher (2009), that it is morally problematic to include only cis women as paradigmatic instances of women (so that trans women would still fall under the term but only as peripheral members of the kind). Given all these difficulties, I do not think that relying only on extensional intuitions regarding gender concepts is a useful methodological approach.

To finish our (brief) discussion of alternative approaches to metaphysical deflationism: Katharine Jenkins (2023) also suggests that to investigate the ontology of gender, one does not need to offer accounts of the application conditions of gender terms. She says:

> it is one thing to try to describe the social reality that explains gender . . . and another thing to try to identify either the meaning of our gender . . . terms or the precise people to whom they apply. Here I'm only engaging in the first of these tasks. In doing so, I use terms like ' . . . gender kinds' to refer to kinds that are intuitively 'in the vicinity of' our . . . gender talk, in the sense that if someone claimed that one of these kinds was the referent of our . . . gender talk, we might agree or disagree, but we would not think that the person was deeply confused or that there had been a fundamental error of communication. To borrow Rowan Bell's evocative phrase, I am concerned with kinds that have '*travelled under the banner of* gender' (Bell 2022, 9, emphasis in original). . . . I intend my usage of terms such as ' . . . gender kinds' to keep open the possibility that only some of these kinds, or indeed none of them, may turn out to be the referents either of our current everyday . . . gender talk or of the . . . gender talk we should be aiming to cultivate. (2023: 117)

In response, I agree that it is useful to think about all those possible kinds that have 'travelled under the banner' of gender, or kinds that are in the vicinity of our gender terms, even if those kinds might not be the actual referents of gender terms (nor the referents that gender terms should have). In this sense, I agree

---

[14] See Byrne (2020) for a philosophical defence of this claim, and Dembroff (2021) for a very compelling rebuttal.

with Jenkins that being open to this possibility is a useful attitude for the metaphysician of gender, since there might be kinds in the vicinity of gender talk that are neither their *actual r*eferents nor the *target* referents, but that are important to investigate for the aims of feminist metaphysics. However, in my view, the phrase 'in the vicinity of gender talk' is not sufficiently clear. Jenkins says that 'if someone claimed that one of these kinds was the referent of our . . . gender talk, we might agree or disagree, but we would not think that the person was deeply confused or that there had been a fundamental error of communication' (117), but unfortunately, I believe that this reaction is very likely to happen, for several candidate meanings for gender terms. For instance, one important point of disagreement in the debate about the nature of gender is whether trans women are women (see Byrne 2020 and Dembroff 2021 for a vivid manifestation of this disagreement). People who believe that trans women are not women and do not fall under the term 'woman', often do say that those of us who believe that trans women fall under the term 'woman' are deeply confused. Moreover, we should keep open about the possibility that those who believe that trans women fall under 'woman', and those who believe that trans women do not fall under 'woman', are using different concepts of woman, and are thus talking past each other, and not really communicating. To give another example, two other important candidate meanings for gender terms have to do with gender as a *social position* (along the lines of Haslanger's account of gender as a social class as stated earlier), and gender as *self-identification* (see Bettcher 2009 and Jenkins 2016 for two compelling defences of the meaning of 'woman' in terms of self-identity). Again, I believe that we should be open to the possibility that different parties in this debate use gender terms with different meanings, and in this sense, they would be talking past each other.[15] Parties in this particular debate would probably not say that the other party is deeply confused, but it is an open position in the debate that the different parties are talking past each other and in this sense, not communicating with each other. Hence, it is not clear to me that the suggested heuristics, having to do with people's intuitions about when users of gender terms are communicating or merely talking past another, is the best strategy to identify the relevant kinds in the vicinity that are worth studying.

As we saw, Jenkins is right that the actual referents of gender terms are not the only focus of interest for the ontology of gender (nor should we limit ourselves to the kinds that gender terms should refer to). However, in my view, if we want to figure out what kinds *have travelled under the banner of* gender terms, the most useful approach is to engage in a two-step inquiry *a la* Thomasson. Among

---

[15] I also make this point in Díaz-León (2018) and Díaz-León (2022).

other virtues, this approach has the promise of telling us which kinds are the actual referents of gender terms, which kinds are the referents the terms should have, and which other kinds may have sometimes been associated with gender terms but are not their current referents. If we dispense with this method, then we are going to be pretty unsure about what kinds have really travelled under the banner of gender terms, since the starting data we have is full of recalcitrant disagreements, and in particular, some speakers will be happy to say that other speakers using gender terms in different ways are deeply confused. Given this situation, I submit, the two-step inquiry offers a systematic approach, a useful method, and a way to make progress in an otherwise intractable debate.

5 The Meaning of Gender Terms I: Amelioration

In order to make progress in the metaphysics of gender, then, we need to investigate the meaning of gender terms (both the actual meanings and the target meanings). This is the question that we will focus on in the following two sections. Firstly, in this section we will review some ameliorative proposals about what gender terms should mean that have been influential in the literature. Secondly, and taking that dispute into account, I will explore two different accounts about what gender terms actually mean, based on two different frameworks in semantics, namely, a contextualist view and an externalist view about meaning (Section 6). And finally, we will draw some conclusions, both about what gender terms are likely to mean, and what we can establish about what they should mean.

As we saw earlier, one of the first advocates of an ameliorative strategy in philosophy of gender was Haslanger's (2000) groundbreaking article. In that article, Haslanger developed not only a new strategy to pursue questions of the form 'what is X?', namely, an ameliorative strategy focusing on what term 'X' should mean, but also a specific account of what gender terms should mean, to wit: an ameliorative account of both the concept of gender and two core gender categories, namely, 'man' and 'woman'.[16] Let's rehearse the ameliorative proposals here for convenience:

> A group G is a gender (in context C) iff$_{df}$ its members are similarly positioned as along some social dimension (economic, political, legal, social, etc.) (in C) and the members are 'marked' as appropriately in this position by observed or imagined bodily features presumed to be evidence of reproductive capacities or function. (2003: 8)

---

[16] Haslanger (2000) does not include the category *of genderqueer*. It might be argued this omission is a form of exclusion, but as Haslanger (2020) makes clear, her main aim in (2000) was to offer an account of gender that would emphasize the injustice and oppression that are operative at the heart of gendered social practices, and we can now see that one form that this oppression takes involves the invisibility of non-binary people. See Dembroff (2018, 2020) for further discussion.

S is a woman (in context C) iff$_{df}$ S is systematically subordinated along some dimension (economic, political, legal, social, etc.) (in C) and the members are 'marked' as a target for this treatment by observed or imagined bodily features presumed to be evidence of a female's reproductive biological role in reproduction.

S is a man (in context C) iff$_{df}$ S is systematically privileged along some dimension (economic, political, legal, social, etc.) (in C) and the members are 'marked' as a target for this treatment by observed or imagined bodily features presumed to be evidence of a male's reproductive biological role in reproduction. (2000: 39)

Haslanger (2000) (and in subsequent work) made clear that these accounts of gender concepts do not intend to capture the ordinary concepts associated with our gender terms. These accounts are not based on an exploration of our intuitions, nor how we would be disposed to apply the terms in different thought experiments. These accounts are useful, Haslanger (2000) argues, because they help us make salient the ways in which human beings are marked for different treatment in virtue of being perceived or imagined to have bodily features presumed to be evidence of a male or female reproductive role.

In addition, Haslanger (2000) was also interested in dealing with the so-called 'commonality' problem, which was very influential in feminist philosophy in the previous decade. The commonality problem is the problem of finding a property or feature that all women have in common, given intersectionality. That is, once we acknowledged that women's social position varies a lot depending on other social identities they instantiate, such as race, class, nationality, sexual orientation, and disability status, it becomes very difficult to identify womanhood with a specific social role, as the classical sex/gender distinction would attempt to do. In response to the difficulties, Haslanger (2000) defended her ameliorative account, where womanhood was defined not in terms of any specific social position or social role that women tend to instantiate, but rather in terms of a very schematic, hierarchical social structure around which human beings are socially positioned, depending also on many other social identities. But Haslanger's crucial idea is that it is possible to identify *women* with the group of individuals who are in a social position of subordination with respect to men, along some axes of oppression, which can include some or many of the following: economic, cultural, legal, social, political, and so on. For example, heterosexual white middle-class women are likely to be economically advantaged with respect to, say, lesbian working-class women of colour. However, they are all women because they all occupy a position of subordination along some axes of oppression (although this account also helps us understand the way different identities intersect to explain further privilege or subordination within the social matrix). It could be argued that not all women occupy a position of subordination along some axes of oppression with respect to men, and therefore, they would not count as women in Haslanger's view. In response to this, Haslanger could bite the bullet and say that her account is supposed to be revisionary. However, it could be argued that Haslanger's account is also extensionally adequate since it does classify all those individuals that we would intuitively count as women, as women. For example, it could be argued that the late Queen of England was not subordinated along any axis of oppression with respect to men, since she was extremely wealthy, had political influence, and so on. We could say in response that even the Queen of England was subject to gendered norms of appearance and behaviour that, say, the current King of England is not subject to.[17]

This defence of ameliorative proposals about the meaning of gender terms gives rise to the important question of what ameliorating the meaning of our terms requires. There has been an explosion of literature on the mechanisms of amelioration or conceptual engineering (see Cappelen 2018 and the multitude of articles on the foundations of conceptual engineering that have appeared recently).[18] For our purposes here, we do not have to go into the details of this interesting, growing debate, but it will be useful to make a couple of clarifications. First, when we talk about ameliorating (or revising) the meaning of a term, we are referring primarily to changes of the *intension* and/or *extension* of the term. The extension is the class of things that fall under the term. The intension is a function from possible worlds (or scenarios, or situations) to the different extensions that the term would have in those possible worlds. For instance, the terms 'cordates' and 'renates' have different intensions (or membership conditions) but they happen to have the same extension in the actual world (since all creatures with a heart have kidneys and vice versa). In most cases, if we change the intension, this will likely change the extension in the actual world, but sometimes a change of intension might not entail a change of extension (when the new intension happens to yield the same extension in the actual world). Given this, I will understand amelioration as the change of intension and/or extension.

Hence, we could understand Haslanger's proposal to ameliorate the meaning of gender terms, as a proposal to revise the *intension* of terms such as 'man' and 'woman'. However, more recently, Haslanger has advocated for a different interpretation of her ameliorative accounts, as follows. Haslanger (2006) argued that the accounts of gender (and race) that she defended in her (2000) article

---

[17] See Jones 2013 for further discussion.

[18] See for instance the articles included in Burgess, Cappelen, and Plunkett (eds.) (2020), as well as many recent articles included in special issues on conceptual engineering published in *Inquiry* and elsewhere.

might actually correspond to the objective types that our gender (and race) terms have been tracking all along. As she explained in (2000) and again in (2006), we should distinguish between the *manifest* concept, that is, the concept that we take ourselves to be using (what we would answer if we were asked 'what is X?'), and the *operative* concept, that is, the concept of the objective type that our usage of term 'X' actually tracks. Haslanger (2006) relies on an externalist framework in philosophy of language to make explicit the idea that competent users of a term do not have to know the underlying nature of the kind, even if they are able to successfully refer to it. Likewise, she argues, gender terms might refer to social kinds even if competent speakers have false beliefs about the nature of their referents, such as the belief that the kinds are biologically significant kinds. Haslanger proposes a version of what she calls 'objective type externalism' according to which externalism is not only plausible with respect to natural kind terms but also with respect to social kind terms, since these also refer to objective kinds.[19] The thought, then, is that gender terms might track the structural social kinds that she identified in her (2000) piece, even if this is contrary to our intuitions, since according to externalism, the referents are not fixed by the intuitions associated with the terms, but rather by external factors that are 'outside our heads'.

Once Haslanger (2006) opened space for this new position according to which our gender terms might refer to the hierarchical social kinds that she had identified in earlier work, the defence of Haslanger's version of social constructionism about gender did not rely only on the possibility of ameliorating or revising the meaning of gender terms. Social constructionism about gender is now an open position about the actual referent of gender terms. Of course, social constructionism does not seem to capture the *manifest* concept of many users of gender terms, but as Haslanger (2006) explains, drawing on classical externalism (by philosophers of language such as Kripke 1972 and Putnam 1973), the manifest concept and the operative concept can come apart, since the operative concept is not fixed by the information in our minds. (In Section 6 we will assess several views about what the *operative* concept of gender might actually be, and in particular in Section 6.2 we will further explore the externalist framework as applied to gender terms. But before turning to that, in the remaining of this section we will explore two other *ameliorative* accounts of what gender terms *should* mean that are different from Haslanger's, which will then be useful as a contrast with respect to the results of descriptive inquiries into the meaning of gender terms in Section 6.)

---

[19] I further spell out objective type externalism in Section 6.2.

Jenkins (2016) offers a very interesting critique of Haslanger's (2000) ameliorative proposal about gender terms. Jenkins' main objection is that Haslanger's ameliorative account of 'woman' earlier does not include all trans women in its extension, and hence, the account is flawed because of this. Jenkins argues that although there are trans women that would clearly fall under Haslanger's account of 'woman', namely, those who are perceived or imagined to have bodily features presumed to be evidence of a female biological role in reproduction, there are other trans women that would not fall under the account, because they would not pass as cis women, that is, they would not be perceived or imagined to have a female role in reproduction. There are trans women who suffer from stigma and abuse precisely because they are perceived as not being biologically female, and this is what explains why they are discriminated in the ways they are. Hence, many trans women are not perceived or imagined to have bodily features that are presumed to be evidence of a female biological role in reproduction, and hence, even if they do occupy a social position of oppression along the axes of oppression that Haslanger mentions, they are not marked as being appropriately positioned *in virtue of* being so perceived or imagined.[20] Hence, they would not satisfy Haslanger's account and they would not count as falling under the extension of 'woman'. As Jenkins argues in a very compelling manner, this is contrary to the feminist aim of mitigating the subordination of trans women and doing justice to the aims of trans women of being recognized as women and living their lives with dignity and respect.

In reaction to this problem, Jenkins (2016) advocates for a different ameliorative strategy regarding the usage of gender terms. Jenkins argues that there are two concepts of gender that are equally useful for the purposes of feminist philosophy. One is the concept of gender as a social class, and it corresponds to Haslanger's account of gender in terms of a social hierarchy. The other is Jenkins' proposed concept of gender as identity, which she defines as follows:

---

[20] Jenkins introduces an interesting distinction between two ways trans women may not fall under Haslanger's account of 'woman', both of which would be a flaw for a proposed ameliorative account of gender terms. First, some trans women are perceived or imagined as not being biologically female, and are discriminated because of this in transphobic contexts which are sadly very common. Second, in some trans-friendly contexts, some trans women might be recognized as trans women, and treated accordingly (by using their preferred pronouns, appropriate gender terms, and so on), but they may still not be perceived or imagined to have a female biological role in reproduction (because people around there would perceive them as trans women, who are fully women for all legal purposes but do not have a female role in reproduction, e.g., they cannot get pregnant nor breastfeed). Jenkins' point is that trans women would not count as women on Haslanger's account in any of these scenarios, not even in the latter one which is supposed to be more trans-inclusive. This shows that Haslanger's account of 'woman' does not apply to many trans women, not even those who inhabit spaces that are more trans-inclusive and are treated as women (by using their preferred pronouns and so on).

> S has a gender identity of X iff S's internal 'map' is formed to guide someone classed as a member of X gender through the social or material realities that are, in that context, characteristic of Xs as a class.

This means that having a female gender identity works as follows:

> S has a female gender identity iff S's internal 'map' is formed to guide someone classed as a woman through the social or material realities that are, in that context, characteristic of women as a class. (410)

The idea here is that to have a gender identity as a woman is a matter of having an internal map (or a global mental state), where one takes the social norms and expectations that are associated with being a woman in that social context, as being relevant to oneself. This is compatible with the subject not wanting to follow those social norms, or the subject not being expected by others to follow those gender norms. What matters for gender identity is whether the subject takes the norms to be relevant to oneself or not.

How should we use gender terms, then, according to Jenkins? She argues that both concepts are essential, but as we can see, the concept of gender identity is defined in part by appealing to the concept of gender as a social class. That is, the concept of gender identity is defined in part by how the subject identifies and locates herself with respect to external social structures that are not within the control of the subject herself. Jenkins suggests that in most contexts, we should use the term 'woman' as referring to subjects' gender identities, although in some contexts it might be useful to use it as referring to gender as a social class.[21] However, it is useful to see that in order to understand gender identity, we need to understand gender as a social class. This already explains why the two concepts are important, even if someone believes that we should always use the term 'woman' as referring to gender as identity.

One of the main reasons for recommending a revision of the meaning of the term 'woman' so that it captures people's gender identities is the problem of the exclusion of trans women, as Jenkins explains.[22] This is a central question in the debates about the amelioration of 'woman'. An interesting, unexplored question is whether we could modify Haslanger's account of gender as a social class so that it becomes more trans-inclusive. One suggestion is mentioned by Jenkins herself (2016: 400, fn. 14) who suggests, drawing on Julia Serano (2007), an alternative account of gender as a social class, where people occupy a certain social position and are marked as appropriately in that position, not in virtue of

---

[21] Jenkins says: 'Imagine a context where trans identities where respected ... Against this background ... the term 'women' could, in my view, safely be used to refer to people classed as women' (2016: 419).

[22] See also Kapusta (2016) for a compelling discussion of the harms of misgendering.

their perceived or imagined bodily features presumed to be evidence of their biological role in reproduction, but rather in terms of expressing femininity. If gender is identified with a social position characterized in this alternative way, then many trans women who are not perceived as having a female role in reproduction, but who are perceived as expressing femininity, would fall under the extension of the term 'woman'. However, this account would not be fully inclusive, because it would not account for trans women who are not 'out' as trans women (and do not have a feminine gender expression due to the transphobia in their environment). Also, it would not include women (either cis or trans) who do not have a feminine gender expression for any other reason. In any case, this point can help us see that there are further options to characterize gender as a social class in terms of a social position in a social matrix, and that Haslanger's account in terms of being marked in virtue of perceived or imagined bodily features presumed to be evidence of biological role in reproduction is only one option among many. Other options might include being perceived or imagined as having a certain gender identity; or being perceived or imagined as having a certain gender expression. Nonetheless, there will always be a gap between characterizations of gender as a *social class* (which depends on someone's social position in a social matrix, which is due to external factors) and characterizations of gender as *self-identity* (which depends on the subject's psychological states). Hence, Jenkins is right that a plausible ameliorative account of gender terms needs to posit (at least) two different concepts, namely, gender as a social class (however it is characterized) and gender as identity.

Talia Bettcher (2009, 2013) has also offered a critique of ordinary usage of the term 'woman' and has recommended a revisionary account of how we should use gender terms. She argues that our current linguistic practices of usage of gender terms are wrong and harmful and should be radically transformed. In particular, she argues that gender terms in our linguistic communities (at least in Western societies) have the aim of revealing someone's genital status, and that this practice is wrong because it is intrusive and attempts to reveal something that should remain private. Bettcher's central idea here is powerful and true, I believe. This is a useful way of reconstructing her main line of thought. Our natural languages include gender categories such as 'man' and 'woman', plus other gendered terms including gender pronouns (and other gendered markers in many natural languages, such as the endings of many nouns and adjectives in Latin languages such as Spanish and French). These gendered expressions are very predominant in European languages such as English and beyond. And, Bettcher argues, this linguistic practice is clearly problematic. Why should we have gendered markers in almost every utterance we make about other human beings? Why should it be the case that every time we want to refer to a human being by using a pronoun, we have to reveal their gender, that is, their genital status? As Bettcher argues, this linguistic practice attempts to track the person's genital status for almost every utterance about that human being, which is clearly intrusive, making something public that should remain private. No matter what topic we are talking about, language forces us to reveal the person's genital status. This is intrusive and unnecessary. I completely agree with Bettcher. Someone could disagree that gender terms in our ordinary practices really aim to reveal genital status. It could be argued that in mainstream linguistic practices, gender terms aim to reveal someone's biological sex, which is not identical to genital status. Even if this is true, there is a correlation between biological sex and genital status. We can understand biological sex as a *cluster* of biological and anatomical features such as chromosomes, internal sex organs, external genitalia, hormonal levels, secondary sex characteristics, and so on. Still, it is clear that to have markers in most of our utterances about human beings that attempt to track human beings' biological sex, no matter what topic we are talking about, is unnecessary, intrusive, breaking privacy rules, and generally unjustified. We should get rid of these practices. Bettcher (2013) argues that we should rather adopt the patterns of usage of gender terms that are already common in trans-friendly communities, namely, to use gender terms to refer to people's gender identities, not to attempt to track people's biological sex.

To conclude: Both Jenkins' and Bettcher's arguments have been very influential in the recent debates about the amelioration of gender terms and the problem of inclusion. They both point to a similar direction: we should use gender terms such as 'woman' and 'man' so that they respect people's gender identities. This view is now widely accepted in feminist philosophy. And as Jenkins (2016) also emphasizes, the notion of gender as a social class is equally indispensable for feminist theory. Remember that in order to spell out gender as identity, we need to appeal to the notion of gender as a class (because Jenkins' characterization of gender as identity appeals to the notion of the social norms and expectations that are part of the social matrix that we are part of, and that we take to be relevant to ourselves, even if other people do not try to enforce those norms onto us). Given this discussion, we can conclude that there are two different concepts that are indispensable for an ameliorative project regarding gender terms: gender as a social class and gender as identity. As we have seen, both Jenkins and Bettcher argue that we should use the term 'woman' to refer to someone's gender identity. I have also argued that there are alternative characterizations of gender as a social class that are more inclusive of trans women, and therefore these alternative accounts should also be taken into consideration. To sum up: if questions in the metaphysics of gender have to do with which concepts of gender we *should* use, then we have now made progress with respect to this question.

6 The Meaning of Gender Terms II: Descriptive Questions

What should gender terms mean? In order to evaluate answers to this question, it is also useful to try to figure out what gender terms actually mean, for some of the considerations that are relevant for evaluating ameliorative proposals have to do with how far from the ordinary meaning we would need to depart. That is, one of the problems that the ameliorative proposals discussed in the previous section have to face is the problem of departing too much from ordinary meaning. If those ameliorative proposals are too revisionary, then it will be difficult to convince people that they have to revise their patterns of usage, and to get them to actually implement those semantic changes.[23] But are those proposals really that revisionary? As I explained in the previous section, Haslanger (2006) argued that there is room for the view that the objective types our gender terms have tracked all along actually correspond to the social kinds that she identified in her (2000) original piece (stated earlier). But on this view, it is the *operative* concepts (that is, the objective types picked out by the terms) that correspond to those social kinds, not the manifest concepts. In Haslanger's (2006) view, the *manifest* concepts that most speakers associate with gender terms are such that they presuppose that the referents are biologically significant. On this view, amelioration still has an important role to play, but the role would be to help us shift the manifest concepts so that they correspond with operative concepts, that is, so that they are in sync. Haslanger (2020) calls this *epistemic amelioration*, that is, the task of better grasping the nature of the content of a concept (that is, to better grasp the operative concept that we actually employ), as opposed to the project of *semantic amelioration*, which is the task of revising the meaning or the content of a term, that is, to change the objective type it picks out. In the spirit of epistemic amelioration, in this section I am going to explore two different theories about what gender terms *actually* mean, and this will help us draw some final conclusions about what gender terms *should* mean.

6.1 Contextualism

How can we approach the question of what gender terms actually mean? A first caveat has to do with the distinction between the manifest and the operative concept that we have already explained. The ultimate aim when we inquire into

---

23 This is similar to the *implementation challenge* as discussed by Cappelen (2018) and elsewhere.

the ordinary meaning of gender terms is to reveal the operative concept, that is, the objective type that is picked out by the corresponding term (if any). However, as we saw in Section 5, there is disagreement among scholars about what the best approach to questions about the operative concept is. On the one hand, *internalist* theorists tend to believe that we need to figure out at least some of the information associated with the term by competent speakers, since this plays a role in fixing the referent of the term. As we saw earlier, scholars that favour this approach include Jackson (1998), Chalmers (2002), Thomasson (2008), Glasgow (2009), and Plunkett (2015), among others. On the other hand, this approach is in contrast with an alternative approach, namely, *externalism*. On this view, referents are fixed not by what is in our heads, but rather by external factors, including environmental factors and causal-historical factors that most competent speakers do not have access to.

As I suggested earlier, in this Element I aim to be as conciliatory as possible with regard to this debate. I agree with advocates of externalism that, given the problem of ignorance and error, it is very difficult to discover any identifying information in our heads that could be part of the meaning, since competent speakers are usually ignorant or mistaken about identifying information about the referent. On the other hand, I agree with the proponents of internalism that it is very difficult to explain reference-fixing without any appeal to information about the referent that is somehow associated with our terms. Given these competing reasons, I will conclude that there is a very modest, but indispensable, role played by information associated with the term regarding reference-fixing. At a minimum, many terms are associated with sortal information about the sort of thing that the referent belongs to.[24] Sometimes we can identify at least some necessary conditions or some sufficient conditions for something to fall under the concept. This minimal stance is still compatible with different semantic approaches.

Often, scholars attempting to reveal the ordinary meaning of gender terms start with some basic intuitions or some basic facts about patterns of usage of gender terms, and they use these starting points to build their theories. In this section I will explore some of these approaches. For instance, Jennifer Saul (2012) starts her investigation by stating that people seem to use gender terms such as 'man' and 'woman' in different ways. Some utterances seem to be about someone's biological sex, whereas other utterances are clearly not about someone's biological sex. She also mentions that according to many feminist scholars, what determines being a woman has to do with the subject's social position or social role, not their biological sex. Taking all these data into consideration, she claims that we should appeal to a 'collection of ordinary

---

[24] We will further discuss this *hybrid* view (in contrast with *radical externalism*) in Section 6.2.

usage data' (2012: 200) as a starting point for our theorizing about the ordinary meaning of 'woman', which we can later argue should be revised given ameliorative considerations. Similarly, N. Laskowski (2020) argues that theories about the actual meaning of 'woman' should satisfy what he calls the 'usage constraint', that is, the idea that the theories should do justice to available data about patterns of usage. He also claims that given the best review of the available data, it looks like people in different contexts can use the term 'woman' with different meanings.[25] From a different starting point, Bettcher (2013) also argues that there seems to be a diversity of usages of the term 'woman'. In particular, Bettcher claims that we can identify a dominant usage of the term 'woman', according to which the term 'woman' aims to refer to someone's genital status (which is a linguistic practice that perpetuates transphobic ideology), and a *resistant* usage of 'woman', which is common in transfriendly communities, where the term 'woman' aims to refer to people's gender identities, and where both cis women and trans women can be paradigmatic instances of women.

In reaction to this appearance of diversity of usages, Saul (2012) introduced a version of contextualism about the meaning of 'woman', as a possible view that could aim to accommodate the apparent diversity of usages. However, Saul (2012) found the view ultimately problematic and did not endorse it. But the reason for not endorsing it was *normative*, not descriptive. That is, Saul (2012) argued that contextualism cannot do justice to the claims of trans women, and for this reason should be rejected. Saul herself acknowledged that this consideration pertains to *ameliorative* projects rather than *descriptive* projects. As we saw earlier (drawing on Haslanger, Dembroff and others), what gender terms actually mean and what they should mean could come apart. But in order to settle this debate, it will be useful to review in more detail some of the literature on what gender terms actually mean, to see if we can make some progress. In particular, we will review two central semantic theories: contextualism and externalism, as applied to gender terms. In this section we will explore the prospects of contextualist theories of the meaning of 'woman', since, as many authors have suggested, it seems, prima facie, that people use the term 'woman' with different meanings in different contexts.[26]

---

[25] In particular, Laskowski (2020) argues that a polysemy account can better account for the available data than a contextualist view. I do not have space to evaluate this debate in detail.

[26] As we saw in Section 4, Dembroff (2018) and Barnes (2020) both suggest that gender terms might change their meaning from context to context, or at least, that there is no unique meaning of gender terms, but rather a plurality of gender kinds in the vicinity of gender talk. Jenkins (2016, 2023) is also sympathetic to a plurality of gender kinds. Given this support for a variety of usages of 'woman', it makes sense to explore a contextualist view, even if very few feminist philosophers fully endorse the view.

Saul's contextualist proposal goes as follows:

> X is a woman is true in a context C iff X is human and relevantly similar (according to the standards at work in C) to most of those possessing all of the biological markers of female sex. (2012: 201)

Recall that Saul's aim is to put forward for our consideration a putative account of the ordinary meaning of 'woman' that can capture the apparent diversity of usages. This version of contextualism is at least prima facie well suited to do that. The account claims that utterances of the form 'X is a woman' have the following truth conditions: the utterance is true if and only if X is human and relevantly similar to most of those that, it is assumed, are paradigmatic cases of being a woman, namely, those who possess all of the biological markers of female sex. This view does not presuppose any specific account of what biological sex is, but it does assume that those who possess all of the biological markers of female sex will probably be paradigmatic instances of women.[27] It is important to bear in mind that according to standard accounts of biological sex, it is not necessary to have *all* the markers of female sex in order to count as being biologically female, only many or most of those markers.[28] Moreover, this contextualist account allows that someone can be a woman even if they do not have many of the biological markers of female sex. How? Because what determines that someone falls under 'woman' is not whether they possess the biological markers of sex, but rather whether they are relevantly similar to those who possess all of the biological markers. Saul's intention, then, was to sketch a view of the meaning of 'woman' that would characterize its meaning in terms of similarity with paradigmatic cases of the referent. This is a common semantic strategy. What makes this view a version of contextualism is that on this view, what counts as *relevantly* similar to those paradigms can vary from context to context. That is, the criteria of similarity can vary from context to context.

Let's consider two different examples to see how the theory would work. In a context of a trans-inclusive feminist conference where someone is taking attendance and keeping a register of the number of women attending the conference, utterances of the form 'X is a woman' express the proposition that X is similar to most of those possessing all the markers of female sex

---

[27] As we saw earlier, Bettcher (2013) suggests that there are resistant linguistic practices involving the term 'woman' where trans women could also count as paradigmatic cases. I think Saul's approach is compatible with this: Saul's strategy only assumes that those who have all markers of female sex are paradigmatic instances of women, not that they are the only paradigmatic instances. In any case, it would be interesting to explore the prospects of alternative versions of contextualism where the paradigmatic instances to which X has to be relevantly similar are inclusive of trans women.

[28] See Stein (1999) and Fausto-Sterling (2000) for very useful surveys of conceptions of biological sex, plus a defence of the cluster account.

(from now on, those who are biologically female, for short) with respect to the criterion of self-identifying as a woman. A caveat: not all those who are biologically female identify as a woman. But arguably, many or most of those who are biologically female identify as a woman. Hence, if X is similar to that group in the sense that she also self-identifies as a woman (where X herself can be biologically female or not), then 'X is a woman' will be true. On the other hand, Saul considers the case of a forensic anthropologist who utters the sentence 'this bone belonged to a woman'. In this context, arguably, the relevant criteria of similarity have to do with having certain DNA or being biologically female more generally. Thus, the referent of 'woman' in this other utterance will be different.

Therefore, the contextualist account seems to be able to accommodate our intuitions about different patterns of usage, at least in some preliminary cases. However, Saul (2012) argues that, after reflection, we can realize that contextualism cannot accommodate all the intuitions that a feminist scholar would want to accommodate. In particular, it cannot do justice to the claims of trans women, who would like to advocate for an account of the meaning of 'woman' that includes all trans women. As Saul (2012) explains, contextualism has the consequence that the advocates of trans women would express a trans-inclusive concept of woman in their utterances involving the term 'woman', but unfortunately, the contextualist view also has the problematic consequence that the opponents of trans women would express a trans-exclusionary concept of woman in their utterances involving the term 'woman'. Why? Let me explain. If we apply Saul's contextualist account to a sentence of the form 'trans women are women' uttered by an advocate of trans women, then the sentence will be true because 'women' will refer to the class of humans who are relevantly similar to those who are biologically female, and in this context, given the relevant criteria of similarity, trans women are clearly similar to most of those who are biologically female in the sense of self-identifying as women (or occupying a similar social position). However, if an opponent of trans women utters 'trans women are not women', contextualism would imply that this utterance is also true, since in this context, 'women' would refer to the class of humans who are similar to those who are biologically female with respect to the following criterion of similarity: possessing all the biological markers of female sex. For this reason, Saul argued that we should reject contextualism about 'woman'. But as she explains, this is an *ameliorative* consideration pertaining to what the term *should* mean, not what the term actually means.[29]

---

[29] Hence, there is space to argue that even if Saul's version of contextualism cannot do justice to the central normative considerations, it is in fact a good account of what gender terms *actually* mean. I will not explore this view in what follows.

In response to Saul (2012), in Díaz-León (2016) I argued that there is an alternative version of contextualism about 'woman' that can satisfy two desiderata: it can do justice to the collection of data that is the starting point for a semantic theory of 'woman', and it can be inclusive of trans women at the same time. The key idea is to use a distinction that other advocates of contextualism (about other terms) have used, namely, *attributor contextualism* versus *subject contextualism*. According to attributor contextualism, a term varies its content from context to context, in virtue of *who* utters the term, that is, depending on features of the speaker. Attributor contextualism is a plausible view about the meaning of demonstratives and indexicals such as 'I', 'you', 'here', and 'now'. The referent of different utterances of these terms depends on who is the speaker and other features of the speaker such as their location in time and space. On the other hand, subject contextualism about a term says that the meaning of that term changes from context to context, depending on features of the subject matter of the utterance that can change from context to context. For example, a plausible version of subject contextualism about 'knowledge' would claim that utterances of the form 'S knows that p' express the proposition that the subject S is able to rule out alternatives to p being true, where which alternatives S needs to rule out depends on features of the situation of S herself (not the speaker who utters the sentence). For instance, if S is at the zoo looking at zebras, then in order for the utterance 'S knows that there is a zebra in front of her' to be true, S would arguably need to rule out the alternative that there is a mule painted as a zebra in front of her. That is, her evidence would need to rule out that there is a mule painted as a zebra (her evidence would have to be sufficient to show that what she is looking at is a zebra, not a mule painted as a zebra). In particular, subject contextualism about 'knowledge' claims that *if* S is in an environment where mules painted as zebras are common, then she would need to rule that out, but if she is in an environment where mules painted as zebras are a very remote possibility, then she does not need to rule that out.

In previous work I used this distinction to defend subject contextualism about 'woman' (Díaz-León 2016). It is clear that a version of attributor contextualism about 'woman' is not going to solve the inclusion problem. The reason is that if the reference of 'woman' in different contexts of utterance depends on the beliefs and values of the speaker, then when transphobic speakers utter the term 'woman', it will not express a trans-inclusive concept. However, according to subject contextualism, it does not matter who the speaker is. Going back to the case of 'knowledge', if we are talking about a zoo-goer at a zoo where there are no mules painted as zebras, it does not matter what the speaker has in mind. If they utter 'S knows that there is a zebra in front of her', it can be true even if

S cannot rule out that she is looking at a mule painted as a zebra, regardless of what the speaker believes about what knowledge requires. Given what 'knowledge' means, and what context the subject of utterance S is at (namely a context without mules painted as zebras), the utterance 'S knows that there is a zebra in front of her' will be true.

Likewise, I argued, if different people utter a sentence of the form 'trans women are women' it does not matter what the speakers have in mind. What matters for the truth conditions of the utterance is who are the subjects of utterance (the same for all the speakers) and what are the relevant criteria of similarity in those contexts. I suggested that the relevant criteria of similarity are determined by normative considerations salient in the context, including moral and political considerations regarding how the people that the utterance is about should be treated for the purposes that are salient in that context. Let's examine a few examples in light of these considerations.

Imagine that we are at a clinic where the nurses received a notice asking them to send notifications to women over forty years old asking them to make an appointment for a smear test.[30] Given these instructions, the nurses go through the files, putting aside the files of the people they need to send letters to. In this context, if they utter a sentence of the form 'X is a woman', it can be argued that the relevant criteria of similarity here have to do with having female genitalia. To consider a different example: imagine that we are in North Carolina discussing the infamous 'bathroom bill' that said that only people who were assigned female at birth could use women's toilets. In this context, it is clear that it is morally wrong to exclude trans women from women's toilets. Hence, the relevant criteria of similarity have to do with self-identifying as a woman, not with being biologically female (nor having certain genitalia). Hence, utterances of the form 'X is a woman' in that context will be true to the extent that X is a human and similar to most of those who are biologically female with respect to the criterion of self-identifying as a woman, which is the relevant criterion of similarity in that context.

In Díaz-León (2022) I argued that subject contextualism can help us understand what is at stake in many contemporary debates between trans allies and so-called 'gender-critical feminism'. According to gender-critical feminism, only those who are biologically female occupy the social position of subordination associated with being a woman.[31] In their view, the term 'woman' does and should only refer to those who are biologically female (or at least, those who are perceived to be biologically female and discriminated

---

[30] Here I draw on a similar example discussed by Saul (2012).

[31] See Lawford-Smith (2022) for a pretty exhaustive exposition of gender-critical feminist views.

because of this). They also believe that trans women should not have access to women-only spaces. One of the points of disagreement has to do with the putative truth conditions of the following sentences:

(1) Women are more likely to be subject to strict norms of beauty than men.
(2) Women are likely to be paid less than men for the same jobs.
(3) Women are more likely to suffer domestic violence than men.

Advocates of gender-critical feminism argue that what makes those claims true is a conception of womanhood in terms of biological sex. However, subject contextualism can help us see why this is wrong. According to subject contextualism, the meaning of 'women' in these utterances is determined by the moral and political considerations that are the most relevant in each context. It is clear that in those contexts, the class of people that are likely to be discriminated in those ways include trans women.

Bettcher (2017), Laskowski (2020), and Dan Zeman (2020) have all independently argued that my version of subject contextualism would collapse into a version of *invariantism* about the meaning of 'woman'. The main reason is that given the harms of misgendering, in most or even in all contexts (at least in the actual world), the duty not to misgender others would take priority, and hence, if the truth conditions of utterances of the form 'X is a woman' are determined in virtue of the moral and political considerations that are relevant in the context (as I argued), then in all those contexts, the truth conditions will be the same, namely, the term 'woman' will refer to people who self-identify as a woman. This is a very important challenge to subject-contextualism. In response, in Díaz-Leon (2022) I considered a variety of examples such as the following:

(4) 'We have to call all women over 40 for a smear test' (uttered in the context of the clinic described earlier)
(5) 'This bone belonged to a woman' (uttered by a forensic anthropologist as explained earlier)
(6) Women are more likely to have their symptoms of a heart attack ignored.

My claim is that in these cases (4–6), it is not obvious that moral and political considerations would always select a referent of 'woman' corresponding to the group of people who self-identify as a woman. To clarify: as I said earlier, it is clear that the view that gender-critical feminists defend, namely, a version of invariantism about 'woman' where the term always refers to those who are biologically female, is very implausible, and subject contextualism can explain precisely where that view goes wrong. To wit: in most contexts, the relevant criteria of similarity clearly do not amount to being biologically female (e.g., utterances 1–3). The remaining question is whether a version of invariantism where the term 'woman' always refers to those who self-identify as a woman would be the most plausible consequence of subject-contexualism about 'woman'. And this is not entirely clear. Of course, Bettcher, Laskowski, and Zeman are right that the duty not to misgender is in effect in all contexts. There are moral and political considerations in favour of respecting people's gender identities that are applicable to all contexts. The question is whether, in addition to this, there are additional moral and political considerations that would have to be weighed up against those, so that the overriding considerations could select a different referent for 'woman'. And I believe a case can be made for this (context-shifting) view.

For example, in utterance (5) earlier, it can be argued that the relevant criteria of similarity have to do with having similar DNA. The claim is not that this is the criterion of similarity that speakers would probably have in mind (this is what attributor contextualism would say), but rather that this is the relevant criterion of similarity, given the moral and political considerations that have priority in that context. To repeat: according to subject contextualism, the relevant criteria of similarity that determine the reference of 'woman' at a context are not the beliefs that speakers have in mind, but rather the moral and political considerations that have the most weight in that context, regardless of what speakers have in mind. This is why Bettcher, Laskowski, and Zeman have all argued that the duty not to misgender would yield the same referent in all those contexts. In response, I believe that there could be additional normative considerations to weigh up. To mention one: Wendy Weisberger (2023) explains in an article at CNN that recent archaeological studies of a 90,000-year-old skeleton found in the Andes Mountains have shown that the skeleton is actually female, although it was first believed to be male (because the presence of weapons next to the skeleton led archaeologists to assume that the skeleton was male). This indicates that the assumption that men but not women were hunters is mistaken. This example is relevant because it is crucial for the purposes of explaining the misinterpretation of archaeological data, that the skeleton was first thought to be male but DNA testing has confirmed it was female. Hence, with this evidence, we have support for claims such as (7): 'the myth of men as hunters and women as gatherers has been shattered' (as explained in Weisberger's article). In my view, subject contextualism would entail that the term 'woman' as it occurs in (7) refers to those who are biologically female, precisely because this is the relevant criterion of similarity in this context, namely, a context where the aim is to make salient the sexist biases in archaeological studies, and the debunking of sexist myths such as that women were not hunters.

Something similar could be argued about utterance (6) earlier. There is now a consensus that symptoms of a heart attack in women are more likely to be misinterpreted, because in medical school the standard symptoms associated with a heart attack are those that occur more often to men. Again, it could be argued that the relevant moral and political considerations that have the most weight for the purposes of this claim would select as the referent of 'woman' those who are biologically female, or at least those who tend to have symptoms of heart attack associated with those who are biologically female (those two groups do not have to be co-extensional). Crucially, the reason that women's symptoms of heart attacks are not so commonly studied is because they are women.

However, to repeat once more, it would be misguided, as advocates of gender-critical feminism often do, to conclude from these examples that the term 'woman' always refers to those who are biologically female. Subject contextualism shows that there is a plethora of contexts where the relevant criteria of similarity do not have to do with being biologically female (for instance, (1–3) earlier, among many other cases). Indeed, we can plausibly say that in most ordinary contexts, the criterion of similarity that will have the most weight corresponds to self-identifying as a woman. For instance, when we talk about who should have access to women-only spaces such as bathrooms, lockers, and shelters, it is clear that the relevant criterion of similarity has to do with gender identity. However, it is an open question what the relevant criteria of similarity are in cases such as (4–7). Sentence (4) is particularly difficult. It could be argued that it can be time-efficient for the nurses at the clinic to use the term 'woman' to refer to those who are biological female, for the specific purpose of calling those who need to make appointments for a smear test (but not, for instance, when it concerns who should be allowed to use the women's toilets at the clinic, where the relevant criterion is self-identification). But on the other hand, there are also good reasons to hold that in a medical context, clinical practitioners should always use gender terms in a way that is trans-inclusive, so the case regarding (4) is still open for further debate.[32]

---

[32] To clarify: we can distinguish two different questions here. One concerns which words the medical personnel should use when they talk about who should make an appointment for a smear test. Arguably, they should not use the term 'woman'. A different question concerns what the medical personnel would mean *if* they made utterances such as 'all women over 40 should call for an appointment'. Once they have made these utterances, I think subject contextualism would have the consequence that the term 'woman' in those utterances would refer to individuals with vaginas. Recall that subject contextualism is a view about the meaning of 'woman' according to which the term refers to those who are *similar* to the paradigms, where the similarity criteria change from context to context, depending on features of the subject of the utterance. Hence, if the medical staff used the term 'woman', the context would select that referent, according to subject contextualism. Another question, as I said, is which terms they should have used (e.g., 'women' versus 'people with vaginas'). Thanks to Matt Cull for pressing me on this. For further discussion, see Freeman & Ayala-López (2018) and Freeman & Stewart (2022).

Much more would need to be said to settle this matter. My main aim in this section is to argue that subject contextualism can illuminate what is at stake in those debates and can help us make progress. Questions about the referent of 'woman' in utterances in different contexts can be understood as questions about what criteria of similarity should have the most weight in different contexts, given the moral and political considerations regarding the subjects of those utterances that have priority in those different contexts.[33] On this interpretation of the debate, it is clear that invariantism according to which 'woman' always picks out those who are biologically female is a non-starter.

Subject contextualism about the meaning of a term is a semantic theory about the term that posits two aspects of meaning, namely, the *character* and the *content* of the term. The *character* is the function or description that is conventionally associated with the term, and that states how the referent of the term is determined in different contexts, given the factors in the contexts that are responsible for determining the referent, which can vary from context to context. The *content*, on the other hand, is the referent that the term would have in each context. According to contextualism, the character associated with a term is fixed by convention, and the content can change from context to context (given that the relevant factors change from context to context). In this section I have explored subject contextualism as a theory about the ordinary meaning of 'woman'. Some reasons in its favour include the idea that many ordinary concepts are defined in terms of some paradigmatic instances and some

---

[33] Chen (2021b) argues that subject contextualism, as I have characterized it, seems to be committed to a form of *moral realism*, since in Díaz-León (2016) I said that the normative considerations that are relevant to fix the referent of 'woman' in each context amount to *objective* features of the subject of the utterance. It is true that moral realism about those normative considerations, specially the moral and political considerations, would be a good fit with subject contextualism. Because *if* moral realism was true, *then* in an utterance of the form 'X is a woman' in a context C, the term 'woman' would refer in C to the group of individuals who are similar to the paradigms, where the criteria of similarity are fixed by the moral and political considerations having to do with X and how X should be treated for the purposes related to the subject matter of the utterance. However, I do not agree that subject contextualism *requires* moral realism. Moral realism might make subject contextualism *simpler*, but I do not see it as a requirement. If some form of non-realism about the moral realm was true, such as relativism or non-cognitivism, then we should understand normative claims accordingly. If, say, relativism about the moral were true, then the referent of 'woman' at a context would be determined by the normative claims that are true in that context (or true according to the standards that are applicable in that context). Does this mean that Saul's worries about contextualism appear again? That is, maybe this means that an utterance such as 'Charla is a woman' would be false in the context of a transphobic community (where Charla is a trans woman who has not had gender reassignment treatment), since the referent would be fixed via normative considerations that assume the standards of transphobic people. Well, in that case, I agree that the utterance would be false. But this does not mean that the sentence would be false in the mouths of transphobic speakers. It would be true in the mouths of everyone, given the standards of the pro-trans allies, and it would be false in the mouths of everyone, given the standards of the anti-trans advocates (given moral relativism). I can bite this bullet.

criteria of similarity with respect to the paradigms that can vary from context to context. However, the idea that the varying criteria of similarity depend on moral and political considerations that have the most weight in that context might seem too revisionary. That is, it might be argued that it is implausible that this is what the term 'woman' actually means. Remember, though, that we are interested in the *operative* concept of 'woman', not the manifest concept. It seems clear that the manifest concept associated with the term 'woman' does not correspond to the contextualist view developed in this section. However, there is still space to argue that this view captures the operative concept. Furthermore, it could be argued that even if this view is not plausible as an answer to the descriptive question of what gender terms actually mean, it could be a useful answer to the ameliorative question of what gender terms should mean.

A final clarification is in order: As we have said, contextualism is a semantic view according to which a term has two aspects of meaning, namely, a *character* and a *content*. For many semanticists, this makes contextualism a version of *internalism*, since on this view terms are associated with some information in our heads (i.e., the character) which, together with features of the corresponding context, will yield a content or extension. However, it is important to notice that this is compatible with the claim that the character, even if it is technically speaking 'in our heads', could come apart from the manifest concept (that is, the character would correspond to the *operative* concept, which can then in turn yield different extensions in different contexts).

In any case, in order to have a more exhaustive discussion of the different options, in the next section we are going to explore a different sort of view, namely, *externalist* views of the meaning of gender terms, according to which the operative concepts are not accessible to the subjects, not even in the way the character is associated with the term according to contextualism. It will be interesting to review these externalist approaches, in part to assess to what extent they are compatible with the metaphysical deflationist framework I have been assuming (spoiler: I think they are compatible), and second, to assess whether externalism would yield different results than contextualism with respect to the actual meaning of 'woman' (spoiler: I do not think so).

6.2 Externalism

Externalism is an approach in philosophy of language according to which the meaning of our terms is fixed by external factors that are not accessible to the speakers by introspection. Externalist views are concerned with both the *semantics* (i.e., the semantic content or meaning of terms) and the *meta-semantics* (i.e., the mechanisms that fix the semantic content of terms) of linguistic expressions. One of the best developed defences of externalism as applied to the aims of feminist philosophy has been offered by Haslanger (2006, 2020). Haslanger's characterization of externalism goes as follows:

> *Objective type externalism*: Terms/concepts pick out an objective type, whether or not we can state conditions for membership in the type, by virtue of the fact that their meaning is determined by ostension of paradigms (or other means of reference-fixing) together with an implicit extension to things of the same type as the paradigms. (2006: 110)

Haslanger uses the label 'objective-type externalism' to emphasize that the insights of externalism can be applied not only to explain the meaning of natural kind terms, but also to other linguistic expressions including social kind terms and all general terms that pick out an objective type. Externalist views became very influential following the work of philosophers such as Kripke (1972) and Putnam (1973), who defended externalism mostly as applied to natural kind terms, which are terms posited in the natural sciences that purport to refer to underlying theoretical kinds ('water', 'gold', 'tiger', etc.). Haslanger's claim is that these insights would also apply to other kind of terms that purport to track an underlying objective type, whether it has been posited by the natural sciences or not. A central idea of externalism is that the nature of the underlying referent can be discovered only empirically. And Haslanger's point is that in many cases, especially concerning areas of political significance such as race, gender and the family, the empirical disciplines that are in a better position to discover empirically the nature of the corresponding referents are the social sciences. Hence, Haslanger's idea is that when it comes to the philosophical project of asking about the nature of gender and race and other politically significant kinds, our intuitions about the corresponding terms are moot: what matters is what the best empirical theories in the social sciences say about the nature of those referents. And it is plausible that ultimately, the social sciences reveal that the core nature of gender corresponds to people's social position in a social hierarchy (which corresponds to Haslanger's account of gender in her (2000) piece).

Let's examine Haslanger's characterization of objective type externalism in more detail. Her central idea is that the reference of the corresponding terms (including gender and racial terms) is determined by ostension to paradigms plus the implicit assumption that we are aiming to pick out the group of individuals of the same kind, where the nature of this common kind (the kind that unifies all the paradigms) is discovered empirically. As Haslanger emphasizes, it is not necessary that competent speakers are able to state the kind membership conditions. Often, speakers are ignorant or mistaken about the membership conditions and this can be discovered only empirically. However, it might be the case that after empirical investigation, experts find out that the paradigms have more than one type in common. (After all, things are typically similar in many ways.) Haslanger is aware of this problem and deals with it as follows: 'Sets of paradigms will typically fall within more than one type. To handle this, one may further specify the kind of type (type of liquid, type of artwork), or may (in the default?) count the common type with the highest degree of objectivity' (2006: 110). As we have seen, the problem is that the set of paradigms alone will probably not select a unique type as the referent. Hence, if we want to identify the operative concept, we need to pose further constraints. The worry is that if we assume that the concept is already tracking a unique objective type, then the hypothesis that ostension to the paradigms alone is sufficient to fix a unique objective type is flawed. Haslanger is aware of this worry and posits further constraints. First, she points out that the concepts may include some sortal information about the kind of kind the referent belongs to, such as the type of liquid, type of artwork, type of animal, and type of plant. The idea, then, is that the *meta-semantics* would need to invoke this sort of information in addition to other external mechanisms in order to explain reference-fixing. (Haslanger would reject the view that this information is part of the *semantics*, though, but she would accept that it can sometimes be part of the meta-semantics. See Haslanger 2020 for further discussion.) However, Haslanger is sceptical that we often have sortal information associated with the concept. In these cases, the referent will just be 'the common type with the highest degree of objectivity', in the absence of further constraints. But how can we figure out the type (among those that unify the paradigms) that has the highest degree of objectivity?

A crucial question for our purposes in this section is whether the notion of objective type externalism is compatible with the framework of metaphysical deflationism that I rehearsed at the beginning. I think they are clearly compatible. Recall that the version of metaphysical deflationism defended earlier has it that the debates in metaphysics of the form 'What is X?' or 'Are Xs real?' can be solved by means of two stages. First, we need to figure out the *application conditions* associated with the relevant term 'X'. These application conditions can be pretty thin, and often, they will amount to only necessary conditions for something to fall under 'X', or only sufficient conditions (very rarely will we have necessary and sufficient conditions associated with the term by all competent speakers). Now, it is important to realize that Haslanger's sortal information associated with the concept, or even the minimal assumption that the term will refer to 'the common type with the highest degree of objectivity' can be identified with the first stage of Thomasson's two-stage meta-metaphysical framework. That is to say, in order to explain reference-fixing, Haslanger acknowledges that we need to posit some sortal information, or at least the assumption that the corresponding terms purport to pick out the most objective type unifying the paradigms. This is what Thomasson would call 'application conditions'. One discussion that we can put aside is whether these application conditions are part of the semantics or only part of the meta-semantics. What is more crucial for our purposes is to realize that in order to fix the referent, we need to appeal to at least some sort of sortal information or another kind of 'anchorage' mechanism. And then, as Thomasson acknowledged, this information or anchorage can yield different referents in different scenarios. That is to say, with the same sortal information, given that we do not know what the external world is like (this can be discovered only empirically), we can conceive of several scenarios that are compatible with the same sortal information. And then, the empirical sciences can tell us which of those scenarios is real, and hence, what the objective type that the paradigms have in common actually is.

In Haslanger's view, the sortal information (or application conditions, to use Thomasson's term) would not be *non-negotiable* (as Glasgow 2009 put it), but on the contrary, this is something we can and often do negotiate. Thomasson (2008) used to argue that we can discover the application conditions by means of engaging in *conceptual analysis* about the contours of our ordinary concepts. But in more recent work (e.g., Thomasson 2020, 2021), she has changed her mind, and now she is more interested in what the application conditions *should* be (which we can discover by engaging in *conceptual engineering*), not what the application conditions actually are (which is difficult to ascertain and not the most important question anyway).

The next question that we have to face is: how can we discover what the type with the highest degree of objectivity is? How can we assess degrees of objectivity? With respect to this question, Haslanger (2016) has offered a very plausible account. I want to rehearse this account of objectivity, also drawing from other philosophers such as Elizabeth Anderson (1995) and Philip Kitcher (2001). The central idea is that objectivity is a matter of the kinds that are the most explanatorily useful, that is, the kinds that have inductive and predictive potential. This is a big question that we do not have the space to examine in detail, but we can at least sketch the sort of view defended in Haslanger (2016), and which draws from feminist philosophers of science such as Anderson (1995) and Kitcher (2001). The central idea is that when we compare the degree of objectivity (or 'naturalness') of several kinds, what matters is what kinds are the most explanatorily useful given the (legitimate) explanatory aims that we have, that is, given our explanatory needs and purposes. What counts as the most objective type is not a question that is independent from us (as Sider 2011 claims). On the contrary, this view goes, there is no way of assessing degrees of objectivity of different kinds in a way that is mind independent. We need to appeal to our (legitimate) explanatory aims and goals in order to ascertain what kinds are the most explanatorily useful with respect to the explanatory needs that we have, as theorists.[34]

This is how Haslanger (2006) defends the claim that gender terms might refer to the social kinds she identified in Haslanger (2000). Indeed, one could argue that the common type with the highest degree of objectivity concerning gender would probably be a biological kind rather than a social kind. However, once we clarify the picture of objectivity that is relevant here, it is clear that what matters is the theoretical kind that has the most explanatory power with respect to the (legitimate) explanatory aims of our inquiry. And the explanatory aims of feminist inquiry include offering explanations of social reality that can help to explain and resist women's oppression and being conducive to social justice. With respect to these explanatory aims, the kind that has the highest degree of objectivity is likely to amount to something akin to Haslanger's social-hierarchical account of gender.

Our final question is the following: what is the connection between context-ualism and externalism? Do these different semantic frameworks yield different conclusions with respect to the *operative* concept of gender? My answer is that, after reflection, they seem to yield similar results. On the one hand, as we saw in the previous section, *subject contextualism* has it that the referent of 'woman' at a context will be determined by the moral and political considerations regarding how the subjects of the utterance should be treated. On the other hand, in this section we have explored a version of externalism according to which the referent of 'woman' is determined by the most objective type that unifies a set of paradigms, where the most objective type amounts to the type that has the most predictive and explanatory power given our legitimate aims and goals in that inquiry. It is likely, though, that different theorists give priority to different aims and goals. Hence, it might be the case that there are different aims and goals that pull us in different directions, even when all those aims and goals are legitimate aims of inquiry. Hence, it is probable that our descriptive inquiries into the operative concept of gender (both from the perspectives of contextual-ism and externalism) will yield a *pluralist* conception of gender. To illustrate, let's consider again some of the examples we examined in the previous section:

(1) Women are more likely to be subject to strict norms of beauty than men.
(2) Women are likely to be paid less than men for the same jobs.
(3) Women are more likely to suffer domestic violence than men.

---

[34] I further develop this view in Díaz-León (2020a, b).

Regarding these examples, the externalist account would imply that the term 'women' refers to the most objective type unifying the paradigms. But as we have seen, according to a plausible account of what the highest degree of objectivity consists in, those terms will refer to the common type that has the most explanatory and predictive power, given the explanatory aims and goals that we give priority to. And it is clear that the hypothesis that 'women' in those occurrences refers to people who are biologically female is a non-starter, on this account. For belonging to the type 'being biologically female' in itself does not explain why women are subject to norms of feminine beauty, or are paid less for the same jobs, or suffer domestic violence. A better hypothesis, with respect to these *explananda*, amounts to an objective type along the lines of Haslanger's account of gender in terms of a social position in a social hierarchy.

Lawford-Smith (2022) argues that the group of people who suffer the patterns of discrimination associated with being a woman corresponds to the group of people that are biologically female. But this is unjustified. In fact, many individuals, including cis women, trans women, and intersex people perceived as female all suffer similar patterns of subordination and oppression, especially when it comes to norms of feminine beauty, being subject to domestic violence, being excluded from positions of authority in academia, politics, and business, or being paid less for the same jobs. And furthermore, what is relevant according to externalism to determine the referent of 'women' is the question of what common objective types are the most explanatorily useful. And it is clear that the type 'being biologically female' cannot explain why the members of that group suffer those patterns of discrimination, since there are possible worlds where people who are biologically female are not so oppressed. What is explanatorily useful is a matter of the social position in a social hierarchy. With respect to this debate, social kinds are clearly more explanatorily useful than biological kinds.

I also examined other examples earlier where, I submitted, biological kinds seem, prima facie, to be more relevant:

(4) 'We have to call all women over 40 for a smear test' (uttered in the context of the clinic described earlier)
(5) 'This bone belonged to a woman' (uttered by a forensic anthropologist)
(6) Women are more likely to have their symptoms of a heart attack ignored.

The externalist framework would yield a similar conclusion. For example, regarding (5), this is interesting because it is useful to posit a biological kind as the referent of the occurrence of 'woman' in this utterance, precisely in order to explain the sorts of biases and prejudices that were common among archaeologists. The relevant factor is that archaeologists used to assume that a skeleton that was buried next to weapons was male, and this is why it is useful, in order to explain and resist sexism, to emphasize that DNA tests have shown that the skeleton in the Andes Mountains was actually female. This is why the externalist framework entails (in my view) that the occurrence of 'woman' in (5) refers to those who are biologically female. But this is a claim about utterance (5), and in no way can we infer anything about other occurrences of 'woman'. Indeed, a preliminary analysis of these examples points to a *pluralist* conception, according to which different occurrences of the term 'woman' pick out different objective types.[35]

7 Other Metaphysical Accounts

What is gender? In the previous sections we have explored this question through a specific method, namely, analysing (or ameliorating) the meaning of gender terms, and figuring out what entities those terms pick out, given those meanings. In particular, according to metaphysical deflationism, this amounts to the project of discovering or stipulating the terms' application conditions, and secondly, figuring out what entities (or kinds), if any, satisfy those application conditions, and what they are like. In this section I will examine some recent alternative approaches to the metaphysics of gender.[36]

7.1 Witt on Uniessentialism about Gender

Charlotte Witt (2011) begins her discussion by focusing on the question of whether a person would become a different person if they changed their gender, or if their gender had been a different one. Witt is interested in exploring to what extent gender is part of our individual identity. She develops a very clear framework in order to offer an answer to this question, namely, what she calls *uniessentialism*, drawing on Aristotelian metaphysics. The main idea, in a nutshell, is that for an individual to be an individual, over and above the set of parts that constitute the individual, the individual must have a certain property or feature that turns those scattered parts into a unified individual. We can then say that the unifying property is *uniessential* to the individual. For example, a house becomes an individual house, over and above the parts (which could be neatly arranged on the floor before construction without yet constituting an individual house), because it acquires the function of providing shelter. The house is an individual, over and above the parts, because it has the function of giving shelter. It can perform this function better or

---

[35] Jenkins (2023) also defends a pluralist account of gender kinds in the vicinity of gender talk (very compellingly in my view), using a different meta-metaphysical approach. I believe our approaches are complementary. See Section 7.3 for further discussion of Jenkins' pluralist view.

[36] An option I do not discuss explicitly here is anti-realism or eliminativism about gender. See Cull (2019) and Logue (2021) for further discussion.

worse (for instance the windows might be malfunctioning, or the roof might be leaky), but it is a house insofar as it has the function of giving shelter to people. Likewise, a human being is an individual over and above the parts (heart, lungs, liver, etc.) because the human being has several unifying functions that the individual organs do not. That is to say, the human being *qua* living organism is organized through some functions or principles that cause the individual human being to exist, over and above the parts. Furthermore, a person is an individual over and above the parts because the person has a unifying perspective, a self. This self then unifies all the random thoughts and emotions the person might experience.

For Witt, the human being and the person are not the same individual, since they have different functions: the human being has the essential functions of a unified living organism, whereas the person has as an essential function, a unifying perspective or a self. The human being could exist without the person, for instance if the human being was in a deep coma, and the person could exist without the human being, for example if we could transplant the brain into another human being, keeping the same thoughts, memories, and so on, unified by the same self. Given this distinction, Witt wonders: is gender uniessential to either the human being or the person? And it seems that the answer is negative: the human being would be the same living organism even if they underwent gender reassignment treatment; and the person would also be the same person (the same self or conscious perspective) if they underwent gender reassignment treatment. The self or the unifying perspective (that is, the subject of experiences) would not change. How then can we capture the intuition that in some deep sense, the individual might have changed? For Witt, the answer is as follows: in addition to the human being and the person, we can distinguish a third individual, namely, the social individual. This corresponds to the individual agent that is responsive to social norms and is socially positioned given the social norms, practices, and expectations that are operative in their social milieu given their social position. In Witt's view, the human being and the person are not subject to social normativity in the way that the social individual is (for instance, the human being is responsive to biological normativity or functions, which the human being can perform better or worse). And how is this social individual unified? Why is there a social individual, over and above the different social norms and practices? Because of gender, Witt answers. In the same way that providing shelter unifies the parts of the house to form an individual house, gender as a social feature unifies all the social positions and social roles that the social individual occupies. Why? Because all these different social roles that the individual occupies are shaped by gender. No other social role, Witt argues, has the same shaping force: gender is uniessential to the social individual because gender is what unifies all the social roles, and in this way determines the social individual that the person performs. For example, many social roles that we occupy are clearly gendered: being a parent is gendered since the social norms are different depending on the person's gender. Being a professor or a lawyer or a doctor or almost any other profession are all shaped by gender, that is, the social norms that constitute those roles vary in virtue of gender. What counts as a good professor or a good doctor, and what is expected of them, varies a lot depending on the person's gender.

Assuming this framework, Witt is able to clearly articulate the important intuition that many of our social roles are shaped by gender in a fundamental way. As Witt argues, this means that gender is *uniessential* to the social individual, that is, the individual exists as a social individual because of gender as a unifying factor that shapes all the other social roles that the person is expected to occupy. In this way, the claim that gender is uniessential to the social individual becomes a useful way of articulating the intuition that gender is central to our social lives.

Witt's argument is debatable,[37] but my main aim here is not to examine Witt's argument in detail, but rather to assess the benefits of her account of gender, independently of the arguments she provides to support it. In Witt's view, gender is a fundamental social role that shapes all other social roles and social norms that we are subject to, and in this sense, if our gender were different, all the other social roles and social norms that determine the social individuals we are would also change. As I have explained, Witt does not reach this view by means of analysing the meaning of gender terms and examining what they refer to. She starts from a very different approach. We could nonetheless wonder whether her account of gender as a social kind might be compatible with the meta-metaphysical approach we developed in the previous sections, and there is no reason to say that it is not. In particular, someone could wonder about the benefits of ameliorating gender terms so that they might come to express gender concepts that capture Witt's account of gender as an essential feature of social individuals. In addition, someone could wonder whether either contextualism or externalism might be concerned with the sort of social feature of individuals that Witt identifies with gender. It might be the case that on a contextualist account, at least in some contexts, the normative considerations that on subject context-ualism determine the referent of gender terms in a context, might yield a referent for gender terms along the lines of Witt's uniessential account. Moreover, on an externalist framework, someone might wonder whether Witt's characterization of gender might be explanatory useful, at least in some contexts, so that it helps to determine the referent of gender terms. At least, Witt gives us some reasons

---

[37] See Ásta (2012), Cudd (2012) and Mikkola (2012) for comments and objections to Witt's view, plus Witt's responses in Witt (2012).

for why her conception of gender is explanatorily useful: it helps to make sense of the powerful intuition that our gender shapes many of the social roles and norms that we are subject to, and that in some sense, if we had had a different gender, we would be different social individuals.

These considerations seem to strengthen the case for pluralism about gender. And it also helps to make sense of the diversity of accounts in the metaphysics of gender, where many of these different accounts seem to do explanatory work that is useful at least for some goals and purposes that the feminist theorist might have.

7.2 Ásta on Conferred Kinds

Ásta (2018) provides a very useful account of the metaphysics of social reality, by means of offering a detailed account of the nature of social properties, and what makes a property *social*. In particular, she argues, social kinds are social in virtue of something about other people's actions. In a nutshell, Ásta argues that a social property is a social status that is conferred upon an entity or individual (or a group of individuals) by a person or a group of persons who have a position of authority, and where the social status comes with constraints on and enablements to the behaviour of the individual who is so conferred (2018: 2).

Ásta is explicit about the methodology that she uses to arrive at her account of social properties, to wit:

> My methodological approach is to have in sight paradigm cases of social properties and of properties that are not social and then to offer an account that gets the paradigm cases right. I take it that being a president and being popular are paradigm cases of social properties and having red hair is a paradigm case of a property that isn't social. I offer a framework, which I call a 'conferralist' framework, that makes sense of these paradigm cases of social property. (2018: 2)

Ásta makes clear that she is mainly interested in giving an account of the nature of social properties, not an account of the meaning of our terms or the content of our concepts. However, given the meta-metaphysical framework that I developed in the first part of this Element, in order to give an account of what a social property is, the first step would be to figure out the application conditions of terms like 'social property' and related terms, and then to examine what entities, if any, satisfy those application conditions. (There is also room to ameliorate or revise the application conditions of the terms, if these are unclear, indeterminate, or flawed for any other reason.)

What should we make of this methodological difference? One could take an approach along the lines of Plunkett (2015) and Thomasson (2016), and claim that indeed, many debates on the metaphysics of the social are at least in part about what certain terms should mean (or what concepts those terms should express), even if this was not explicit in those projects. Plunkett (2015) and Thomasson (2016) revisit several traditional debates in mainstream metaphysics and argue that those debates could be seen at least in part as debates about what certain central terms should mean, or what concepts should be employed. I am sympathetic to this strategy, but I will not press it further here. Rather, I want to make two different points.

First, Ásta's approach starts from paradigm cases of social properties. This is somewhat similar to Haslanger's externalist approach in Section 6.2, that is, an account for figuring out which kinds or properties our *general terms* pick out (and therefore, an account to figure out the *referent* of certain terms). And as we explained earlier, this is also somewhat similar to Thomasson's two-stage metaphysical inquiry, because Haslanger also emphasizes the need to include some additional information in the form of sortal descriptions (which arguably correspond to what Thomasson calls application conditions, even if minimal). Second, the versions of contextualism about gender terms that we examined in Section 6.1 also appeals to paradigm cases of 'woman', that is, those who have all the markers associated with being biologically female (and then the referent will be fixed by a relation of similarity to those paradigm cases, a relation of similarity which can change from context to context). Hence, there are some methodological similarities among these different approaches, even if one were to reject some of the theoretical assumptions of metaphysical deflationism.

Let's put methodological issues aside and let's have a look at Ásta's conferralist account of social properties, and in particular her account of sex and gender as conferred social properties. Ásta argues that social properties are social statuses that are conferred to someone by others, where those who do the conferring are attempting to track a base property that (they believe) the subject instantiates, but what determines that the subject has the social property is not that base property, but rather the act of conferring the social status upon the subject. Ásta provides a useful schema to capture the different elements of the conferral of a social property, as follows:

> Conferred property: what property is conferred . . .
> Who: who the subjects are . . .
> What: what attitude, state, or action of the subjects matter . . .
> When: under what conditions the conferral takes place
> Base property: what the subjects are attempting to track (consciously or not),
> if anything. (2018: 8)

Let's now look at how Ásta applies this schema to the categories of sex and gender. Ásta makes a distinction between two kinds of social properties: *institutional* and *communal* (2018: 17–18). Institutional categories are those that are conferred by individuals in a position of *authority* in virtue of their place in an institution, that is, those who do the conferring have institutional authority. Some examples include, for instance, being the Prime Minister and being legally married. On the other hand, communal properties are also conferred properties, but they are conferred by people who do not have institutional authority, although some kind of *social standing* is necessary. One example is the property of being cool or being popular.

Ásta then argues that whereas sex is an institutional property, gender is a communal property. Her account of sex as an institutional property goes as follows:

> Property: being female, male [in some jurisdictions, a third sex is possible]
> Who: legal authorities . . .
> What: the recording of a sex in official documents . . .
> When: at birth (in the case of newborns) . . .
> Base property: the aim is to track as many sex-stereotypical characteristics as possible . . . . (72)

And her account of gender is the following:

> Property: being of gender G, for example, a woman, man, trans*
> Who: the subjects with standing in the particular context
> What: the perception of the subject S that the person has the base property P
> When: in some particular context
>
> Base property: the base property P, for example, the role in biological reproduction; in others it is the person's role in societal organization of various kinds, sexual engagement, bodily presentation, preparation of food at family gatherings, self-identification, and so on. (74–75)

As we can see, in Ásta's view, someone's gender as a communal property can vary from context to context, because what property is conferred upon someone by the people who happen to have social standing in a context can vary. (As I understand it: both the people who have social standing, and what status they confer, can vary from context to context.) Ásta mentions several base properties that the people who do the conferring might be attempting to track. The first one sounds similar to Haslanger's account of gender, because it has to do with the perception (right or not) of someone's role in reproduction. But this is not the only 'marker' that matters for the conferral of gender, in Ásta's view.

What should we make of this diversity of genders? I want to make two points. First, Ásta's view also makes someone's gender context-dependent (like subject contextualism in Section 6.1), but for different reasons. Ásta's view is not about the meaning of any particular terms, but rather, a claim about the nature of the conferral mechanisms: she claims that people conferring the social status of gender can be attempting to track different base properties in different contexts. This is not a claim about the meaning of gender terms. However, if one is sympathetic to contextualism about the meaning of gender terms, then one could appeal to Ásta's view, in order to offer further support for context sensitivity. For if there really is such diversity of conferred social statuses as part of our diverse social practices, then it would make sense to appeal to different criteria of similarity in different contexts, when trying to figure out the referent of gender terms, as I explained in Section 6.1 earlier. It is possible to combine a contextualist view about the meaning of gender terms and Ásta's conferralist account of gender as a communal conferred property that can change from context to context.

In Section 6.2 we talked about how different kinds can be explanatorily useful for different purposes, and how this is relevant in order to determine the referent of general terms on an externalist framework (since the kinds that are more explanatorily useful in the vicinity have more chances of being the referent of the term that was introduced by ostension). Given this, and on the face of the diversity of gender kinds that our discussion so far illustrates, we can ask which kinds have the potential of being more explanatorily useful. This is one of the questions that Jenkins (2023) undertakes, as I will explain in the following section

7.3 Jenkins on Gender Kinds for Emancipatory Purposes

Jenkins (2023) is interested in giving an account of social reality that helps to illuminate which gender (and race) kinds are most useful for emancipatory purposes. As a result of her useful exploration of this question, she arrives at three different sorts of gender kinds that are useful for emancipatory purposes. In a nutshell, these are the following: (i) what she calls *hegemonic* kinds (which correspond more or less to Haslangerian social structures such as Haslanger's characterization of gender in terms of the social position of privilege or subor-dination in virtue of someone's perceived or imagined role in reproduction); (ii) what Jenkins calls *interpersonal* kinds (which correspond roughly to Ásta's communal conferred properties, such as her account of gender as a communal property); and (iii) what Jenkins calls *identity* kinds, which include identity kinds in two different senses: First, *identity* in the sense of *norm-relevancy*, which corresponds to Jenkins' (2016, 2018) previous account of gender identity in terms of norm-relevancy (see Section 5), and second, identity in the sense of *self-identification*, which is different from identity as norm-relevancy. (See Jenkins (2023: 158–65) for further discussion.)

Jenkins is concerned with giving a detailed explanation of these different gender kinds because of her aim of offering accounts of social reality that help with emancipatory purposes. In particular, she introduces the concept of ontic injustice, and shows how the different gender kinds that she describes can be helpfully illuminated by means of exploring to what extent they exhibit ontic injustice or not. She characterizes ontic injustice as follows:

> Ontic injustice: An individual suffers ontic injustice if and only if they are socially constructed as a member of a certain social kind where that construction consists, at least in part, of their falling under a set of social constraints and enablements that is wrongful to them. (2023: 24)

The notion of ontic injustice is useful, among other reasons, because it can help us understand what is the kind of wronging that is done to a person by a society that constructs social kinds of that sort. And in turn, she explains how the different sorts of gender kinds that she identifies in her tripartite classification relate to the notion of ontic injustice.

Once again, the question for us, at the end of this arch, is whether the framework that I have developed in this Element can help to guide us around this territory. And I think it has potential. As I have painstakingly emphasized, if we want to answer the question of what gender terms actually mean or should mean, we need to investigate the application conditions that the terms have or should have, and then, what entities or kinds, if any, better satisfy those application conditions. Now we have explored (even if briefly) a rich diversity of accounts about what gender might be (or what gender kinds there might be). In my view, the deflationist framework helps to make sense of this diversity, and additionally, it helps to understand where the disagreement might lie. For example, there might be disagreement at the level of which paradigm cases are selected, or at the level of what application conditions are ascribed to the terms, or at the level of which contexts are selected, or at the level of empirical claims about which entities satisfy certain application conditions, or which kinds are more explanatorily useful. Moreover, there might be disagreement at the level of the normative considerations that we give priority to, at the different contexts, that is, in order to select the paradigms, or to ameliorate the meaning of the terms, or to select the similarity criteria that are relevant in a contextualist account, or to identify the kinds that are the most explanatorily useful in an externalist account. All these choice points lead to a pluralist account of gender kinds.

8 Conclusion

In this Element we have first examined several influential accounts of the meaning of gender terms such as 'woman', under the assumption that debates in the metaphysics of gender are, at least in part, about the meaning that gender terms have or should have. And I have argued that these different accounts all seem to point to a similar conclusion, namely, that gender terms, and in particular the term 'woman', can pick out different objective types in different contexts. Moreover, I have examined several accounts of the metaphysics of social reality and in particular of the metaphysics of gender as part of that social reality, in the form of projects that aim to describe the social reality underlying gender in ways that are useful for emancipatory goals. And again, we have found a diversity of gender kinds that are useful to illuminate. There are different ways of fleshing out this idea, depending on the different starting points or semantic and meta-metaphysical frameworks, but they all seem to have an important tenet in common, namely, the idea that the referent of 'woman' at a context, or for some particular explanatory purposes, is a question that depends on the normative considerations (including moral and political considerations) that we give priority to, or that are more pressing in that context.

As I said at the beginning, the metaphysics of gender is a sub-field of philosophy that has been growing exponentially in the last two decades, and especially in the last few years. There are quite a few works that have appeared very recently or are forthcoming, which promise to be significant contributions to the debate.[38] I did not have the chance to cover all of them, since I have focused mostly on the main moves in the debates during the two decades after Haslanger's (2000) groundbreaking article. I hope that this Element will offer a useful map of the territory, and the necessary background to delve deeper into the newest developments. I also hope that this discussion shows the richness, philosophical sophistication, and political relevance of this sub-field of analytic philosophy.[39]

---

[38] Some important works that have just been published or are forthcoming include: Briggs & George (2023), Cosker-Rowland (2023, 2024), Cull (2024), and Moyal-Sharrock & Sandis (2024).

[39] This research has been supported by grants PID2021-124100NB-I00 and CEX2021-001169-M (funded by MICIU/AEI/10.13039/501100011033). I am very grateful to Mona Simion for organizing a work-in-progress symposium at the Cogito Epistemology Research Centre at the University of Glasgow, and to Matt Cull, Jade Fletcher, Chris Kelp, Lilith Mace, Bryan Pickel, and Mona Simion for their very useful comments on an earlier draft. Extra thanks are also due to two anonymous referees and to the series editor. This Element is dedicated to K.S.A, with love and gratitude.

References

Anderson, E. (1995) 'Knowledge, Human Interests, and Objectivity in Feminist Epistemology', *Philosophical Topics* 23 (2): 27–58.

Appiah, K.A. (1985) 'The Uncompleted Argument: Du Bois and the Illusion of Race', *Critical Inquiry* 12 (1): 21–37.

Ásta (2012) 'Comments on Charlotte Witt, The Metaphysics of Gender', *Symposia on Gender, Race and Philosophy* 8 (2): 1–5. http://web.mit.edu/~sgrp/2012/no2/SGRPv8no2(0512).pdf.

Ásta (2018) *Categories We Live By: The Construction of Sex, Gender, Race, and Other Social Categories*. Oxford University Press.

Barnes, E. (2014) 'Going Beyond the Fundamental: Feminism in Contemporary Metaphysics', *Proceedings of the Aristotelian Society* 114 (3pt3): 335–351.

Barnes, E. (2017) 'Realism and Social Structure', *Philosophical Studies* 174 (10): 2417–2433.

Barnes, E. (2020) 'Gender and Gender Terms', *Nous* 54 (3): 704–730.

Bell, R. (2022) 'Gender Norms and Gendered Traits', PhD Diss., Syracuse University.

Bettcher, T. (2009) 'Trans Identities and First-Person Authority', in L. Shrage (ed.), *You've Changed: Sex Reassignment and Personal Identity*. Oxford University Press, pp. 98–120.

Bettcher, T. (2013) 'Trans Women and the Meaning of "Woman"', in A. Soble, N. Power & R. Halwani (eds.), *Philosophy of Sex: Contemporary Readings*, 6th ed. Rowan & Littlefield, pp. 233–250.

Bettcher, T. (2017) 'Trans Feminism: Recent Philosophical Developments', *Philosophy Compass* 12 (11): e12438.

Briggs, R. A. & B. R. George (2023) *What Even is Gender?* Routledge Taylor & Francis.

Burgess, A. & D. Plunkett (2013a) 'Conceptual Ethics I', *Philosophy Compass* 8 (12): 1091–1101.

Burgess, A. & D. Plunkett (2013b) 'Conceptual Ethics II', *Philosophy Compass* 8 (12): 1102–1110.

Burgess, A., Cappelen, H. & D. Plunkett (eds.) (2020). *Conceptual Engineering and Conceptual Ethics*. Oxford University Press.

Byrne, A. (2020) 'Are Women Adult Human Females?' *Philosophical Studies* 177 (12): 3783–3803.

Cappelen, H. (2018) *Fixing Language: An Essay on Conceptual Engineering*. Oxford University Press.

Chalmers, D. (1996) *The Conscious Mind*. Oxford University Press.

Chalmers, D. J. & Jackson, F. (2001) 'Conceptual Analysis and Reductive Explanation', *Philosophical Review* 110 (3): 315–361.

Chalmers, D. J. (2002) 'On Sense and Intension', *Philosophical Perspectives* 16: 135–182.

Chalmers, D. J. (2009) 'Ontological Anti-Realism', in D. Chalmers, D. Manley & R. Wasserman (eds.), *Metametaphysics: New Essays on the Foundations of Ontology*. Oxford University Press, pp. 77–129.

Chen, H.-Y. (2021a) 'On the Amelioration of "Women"'. *Philosophia* 49 (4): 1391–1406.

Chen, H.-Y. (2021b) 'Contextualism and the Semantics of "Woman"'. *Ergo: An Open Access Journal of Philosophy* 7, 577–597.

Cosker-Rowland, R. (2024) 'The Normativity of Gender', *Noûs* 58 (1): 244–270.

Cosker-Rowland, R. (2023) 'Recent Work on Gender Identity and Gender', *Analysis*, 83 (4): 801–820.

Cudd, A. (2012) 'Comments on Charlotte Witt, The Metaphysics of Gender', *Symposia on Gender, Race and Philosophy* 8 (2): 1–7. http://web.mit.edu/~sgrp/2012/no2/SGRPv8no2(0512).pdf.

Cull, M. J. (2019) 'Against Abolition', *Feminist Philosophy Quarterly* 5 (3): 1–16.

Cull, M. J. (2024) *What Gender Should Be*. Bloomsbury.

Dembroff, R. (2018) 'Real Talk on the Metaphysics of Gender', *Philosophical Topics* 46 (2): 21–50.

Dembroff, R. (2020) 'Beyond Binary: Genderqueer as Critical Gender Kind', *Philosophers' Imprint* 20 (9): 1–23.

Dembroff, R. (2021) 'Escaping the Natural Attitude About Gender', *Philosophical Studies* 178 (3): 983–1003.

Devitt, M. & Sterelny, K. (1999). *Language and Reality: An Introduction to the Philosophy of Language*. MIT Press.

Díaz-León, E. (2016) '*Woman* as a Politically Significant Term: A Solution to the Puzzle', *Hypatia* 31 (2): 245–258.

Díaz-León, E. (2018) 'On Haslanger's Meta-Metaphysics: Social Structures and Metaphysical Deflationism', *Disputatio* 10 (50): 201–216.

Díaz-León, E. (2020a) 'Descriptive vs. Ameliorative Projects: The Role of Normative Considerations', in A. Burgess, H. Cappelen, and D. Plunkett (eds.), *Conceptual Engineering and Conceptual Ethics*. Oxford University Press, pp. 170–186.

Díaz-León, E. (2020b) 'On the Conceptual Mismatch Argument: Descriptions, Disagreement, and Amelioration', in T. Marques & Å. Wikforss (eds.),

Shifting Concepts: The Philosophy and Psychology of Concept Variability. Oxford University Press. pp. 190–212.

Díaz-León, E. (2021) 'Substantive Metaphysical Debates about Gender and Race: Verbal Disputes and Metaphysical Deflationism', *Journal of Social Philosophy* 53 (4): 556–574.

Díaz-León, E. (2022) 'The Meaning of "Woman" and the Political Turn in Philosophy of Language', in D. Bordonaba Plou, V. Fernández Castro & J. R. Torices (eds.), *The Political Turn in Analytic Philosophy.* De Gruyter, pp. 229–256.

Díaz-León, E. (forthcoming-a) 'Analytic Feminism', in M. Rossberg (ed.), *Cambridge Handbook of Analytic Philosophy.* Cambridge University Press.

Díaz-León, E. (forthcoming-b) 'Conceptual Engineering and Conceptual Revision without Changing the Subject: A Haslangerian Account', in M. G. Isaac, K. Scharp & S. Koch (eds.), *New Perspectives on Conceptual Engineering.* Synthese Library.

Epstein, B. (2015) *The Ant Trap: Rebuilding the Foundations of the Social Sciences.* Oxford University Press.

Fausto-Sterling, A. (2000) *Sexing the Body: Gender Politics and the Construction of Sexuality.* Basic Books.

Freeman, L. & Ayala-López, S. (2018) 'Sex Categorization in Medical Contexts: A Cautionary Tale', *Kennedy Institute of Ethics Journal* 28 (3): 243–280.

Freeman, L. & Stewart, H. (2022) 'The Problem of Recognition, Erasure, and Epistemic Injustice in Medicine: Harms to Transgender and Gender Non-Binary Patients –Why We Should Be Worried', In P. Giladi & N. McMillan (eds.), *Epistemic Injustice and the Philosophy of Recognition.* Routledge Taylor & Francis Group.

Garry, A. (2022) 'Analytic Feminism', in E. N. Zalta & U. Nodelman (eds.), *Stanford Encyclopedia of Philosophy* (Winter 2022 Edition), https://plato .stanford.edu/archives/win2022/entries/femapproach-analytic/.

Glasgow, J. (2009) *A Theory of Race.* Routledge.

Griffith, A. M. (2017) 'Social Construction and Grounding', *Philosophy and Phenomenological Research* 97 (2): 393–409.

Griffith, A. M. (2018) 'Social Construction: Big-G Grounding, Small-G Realization', *Philosophical Studies* 175 (1): 241–260.

Haslanger, S. (2000) 'Gender and Race: (What) are They? (What) Do We Want Them to Be?' *Noûs* 34 (1): 31–55.

Haslanger, S. (2003) 'Future Genders? Future Races?' *Philosophic Exchange* 34 (1): 1–24.

Haslanger, S. (2006) 'What Good are Our Intuitions? Philosophical Analysis and Social Kinds', *Proceedings of the Aristotelian Society* 80 (1): 89–118.

Haslanger, S. (2016) 'Theorizing with a Purpose: The Many Kinds of Sex', in C. Kendig (ed.), *Natural Kinds and Classification in Scientific Practice.* Routledge, pp. 129–144.

Haslanger, S. (2018) 'Social Explanation: Structures, Stories, and Ontology. A Reply to Díaz León, Saul, and Sterken', *Disputatio* 10 (50): 245–273.

Haslanger, S. (2020) 'How Not to Change the Subject', in T. Marques & Å. Wikforss (eds.), *Shifting Concepts: The Philosophy and Psychology of Conceptual Variability.* Oxford University Press, pp. 235–259.

Hochman, A. (2019) 'Race and Reference', *Biology and Philosophy* 34 (2): 32.

Jackson, F. (1998) *From Metaphysics to Ethics: A Defence of Conceptual Analysis.* Oxford University Press.

Jenkins, K. (2016) 'Amelioration and Inclusion: Gender Identity and the Concept of *Woman*', *Ethics*, 126 (2): 394–421.

Jenkins, K. (2018) Toward an Account of Gender Identity. *Ergo: An Open Access Journal of Philosophy* 5, 713–744.

Jenkins, K. (2023) *Ontology and Oppression: Race, Gender, and Social Reality.* Oxford University Press.

Jones, K. (2013) 'Intersectionality and Ameliorative Analyses of Race and Gender', *Philosophical Studies* 171 (1): 99–107.

Joyce, H. (2021) *Trans: When Ideology Meets Reality.* Oneworld.

Kapusta, S. (2016) 'Misgendering and its Moral Contestability', *Hypatia* 31 (3): 512–519.

Kitcher, P. (2001) *Science, Truth, and Democracy.* Oxford University Press.

Kripke, S. (1972/1980) *Naming and Necessity.* Harvard University Press.

Laskowski, N. G. (2020) 'Moral Constraints on Gender Concepts', *Ethical Theory and Moral Practice 23* (1): 39–51.

Lawford-Smith, H. (2022) *Gender-Critical Feminism.* Oxford University Press.

Logue, H. (2021) 'Gender Fictionalism', *Ergo: An Open Access Journal of Philosophy* 8: 125–162.

Mason, R. (2021) 'Social Kinds are Essentially Mind-Dependent', *Philosophical Studies* 178 (12): 3975–3994.

Mikkola. M. (2012) 'How Essential is Gender Essentialism? Comments on Charlotte Witt's The Metaphysics of Gender', *Symposia on Gender, Race and Philosophy*, 8(2): 1–10. http://web.mit.edu/~sgrp/2012/no2/SGRPv8no2 (0512).pdf.

Mikkola, M. (2015) 'Doing Ontology and Doing Justice: What Feminist Philosophy Can Teach Us About Meta-Metaphysics', *Inquiry: An Interdisciplinary Journal of Philosophy* 58 (7–8): 780–805.

Mikkola, M. (2016) *The Wrong of Injustice: Dehumanization and Its Role in Feminist Philosophy*. Oxford University Press.

Mikkola, M. (2017) 'On the Apparent Antagonism between Feminist and Mainstream Metaphysics', *Philosophical Studies* 174 (10): 2435–2448.

Mikkola, M. (2023) 'Feminist Perspectives on Sex and Gender', in E. N. Zalta & U. Nodelman (eds.), *The Stanford Encyclopedia of Philosophy* (Fall 2023 Edition), https://plato.stanford.edu/archives/fall2023/entries/feminism-gender/.

Moyal-Sharrock, D. & Sandis, C. (2024) *Real Gender: A Cis Defence of Trans Realities*. Polity Press.

Passinsky, A. (2021) 'Finean Feminist Metaphysics', *Inquiry: An Interdisciplinary Journal of Philosophy* 64 (9): 937–954.

Plunkett, D. (2015) 'Which Concepts Should We Use? Metalinguistic Negotiations and The Methodology of Philosophy', *Inquiry: An Interdisciplinary Journal of Philosophy* 58 (7–8): 828–874.

Putnam, H. (1973) 'Meaning and Reference', *Journal of Philosophy* 70 (19): 699–711.

Richardson, K. (2022) 'The Metaphysics of Gender is (Relatively) Substantial', *Philosophy and Phenomenological Research* 107 (1): 192–207.

Richardson, K. (2023) 'Critical Social Ontology', *Synthese* 201 (6): 1–19.

Saul, J. (2012) 'Politically Significant Terms and Philosophy of Language', in S. Crasnow & A. Superson (eds.), *Out from the Shadows: Analytical Feminist Contributions to Traditional Philosophy*. Oxford University Press, pp. 195–216.

Schaffer, J. (2009) 'On What Grounds What', in D. Manley, D. J. Chalmers & R. Wasserman (eds.), *Metametaphysics: New Essays on the Foundations of Ontology*. Oxford University Press. pp. 347–383.

Schaffer, J. (2017) 'Social Construction as Grounding; or: Fundamentality for Feminists, a Reply to Barnes and Mikkola', *Philosophical Studies* 174 (10): 2449–2465.

Serano, J. (2007) *Whipping Girl: A Transsexual Woman on Sexism and the Scapegoating of Femininity*. 2nd ed. Seal Press.

Sider, T. (2011) *Writing the Book of the World*. Oxford University Press.

Sider, T. (2017) 'Substantivity in Feminist Metaphysics', *Philosophical Studies* 174 (10): 2467–2478.

Stein, E. (1999) *The Mismeasure of Desire*. Oxford University Press.

Stock, K. (2021) *Material Girls: Why Reality Matters for Feminism*. Fleet.

Taylor, E. (2023) 'Substantive Social Metaphysics', *Philosophers' Imprint* 23: 1–18.

Thomasson, A. (2008) 'Existence Questions', *Philosophical Studies* 141 (1): 63–78.

Thomasson, A. (2012) 'Research Problems and Methods in Metaphysics', in R. Barnard and N. Manson (eds.), *The Continuum Companion to Metaphysics*. Continuum, pp. 14–45.

Thomasson, A. (2015) *Ontology Made Easy*. Oxford University Press.

Thomasson, A. (2016) 'Metaphysical Disputes and Metalinguistic Negotiation', *Analytic Philosophy* 58 (1): 1–28.

Thomasson, A. (2017) 'What Can We Do, When We Do Metaphysics?' in G. D'Oro & S. Overgaard (eds.), *The Cambridge Companion to Philosophical Methodology*. Cambridge: Cambridge University Press, pp. 101–121.

Thomasson, A. (2020) 'A Pragmatic Method for Normative Conceptual Work', in H. Cappelen, D. Plunkett & A. Burgess (eds.), *Conceptual Engineering and Conceptual Ethics*. Oxford University Press, pp. 435–458.

Thomasson, A. (2021) 'Conceptual engineering: when do we need it? How can we do it?' *Inquiry*, http://doi.org/10.1080/0020174X.2021.2000118.

Weisberger, M. (2023) 'Shattering the myth of men as hunters and women as gatherers', CNN. www.cnn.com/2023/06/30/world/women-roles-hunter-gatherer-societies-scn.

Witt, C. (2011) *The Metaphysics of Gender*. Oxford University Press.

Witt, C. (2012) 'The Metaphysics of Gender: Reply to Critics'. *Symposia on Gender, Race and Philosophy* 8 (2): 1–10. http://web.mit.edu/~sgrp/2012/no2/SGRPv8no2(0512).pdf.

Zeman, D. (2020) 'Subject-Contextualism and the Meaning of Gender Terms', *Journal of Social Ontology* 6 (1):69–83.

Cambridge Elements

Metaphysics

Tuomas E. Tahko

University of Bristol

Tuomas E. Tahko is Professor of Metaphysics of Science at the University of Bristol, UK. Tahko specialises in contemporary analytic metaphysics, with an emphasis on methodological and epistemic issues: 'meta-metaphysics'. He also works at the interface of metaphysics and philosophy of science: 'metaphysics of science'. Tahko is the author of *Unity of Science* (Cambridge University Press, 2021, *Elements in Philosophy of Science*), *An Introduction to Metametaphysics* (Cambridge University Press, 2015), and editor of *Contemporary Aristotelian Metaphysics* (Cambridge University Press, 2012).

About the Series

This highly accessible series of Elements provides brief but comprehensive introductions to the most central topics in metaphysics. Many of the Elements also go into considerable depth, so the series will appeal to both students and academics. Some Elements bridge the gaps between metaphysics, philosophy of science, and epistemology.

Cambridge Elements ≡

Metaphysics

Elements in the Series

Printed in the United States
by Baker & Taylor Publisher Services